THUNDER IN ITS COURSES

ESSAYS ON THE BATTLECRUISER

The battlecruisers HMS Repulse *and* Renown *with battleships following in line.*

RICHARD WORTH

NIMBLE BOOKS LLC

Nimble Books LLC

1521 Martha Avenue

Ann Arbor, MI, USA 48103

http://www.NimbleBooks.com

wfz@nimblebooks.com

+1.734-330-2593

Copyright 2011 by Richard Worth

Version 1.0; last saved 2011-06-13.

Printed in the United States of America

ISBN-13: 978-1-60888-101-7

CONTENTS

ILLUSTRATIONS

NIMBLE BOOKS LLC

FOREWORD

This set of essays has its origins in the endless wrangling among warship enthusiasts on the subject of the battlecruiser—where it came from, what was wrong with it, and which ships deserved such a rating. Such ardent attention proves that the extinct creature still fascinates, and that solid information is lacking.

At the core of the debates lies a sense of tragedy worthy of the Bard. Battlecruisers entered the world with apparently unsurpassed might, then apparently exited with irreversible shame. Yet the facts are far more interesting than the perceptions. Battlecruisers, though revolutionary, fit snugly into a historical context where their genesis and exodus make perfect sense.

This doesn't mean the topic has no oddities. On the contrary, within the larger story of the battlecruiser, there exist many specific, irksome issues. This book addresses both the fundamentals of the battlecruiser's place in naval history and some isolated curiosities that continue to spark debate, plus a few tidbits of vagrant thought.

In preparing my text, I had help from a number of researchers, including John Roberts, John Jordan, Enrico Cernuschi, Jan Visser, William Jurens, Peter M. Kreuzer, Zvonimir Freivogel, John Brooks, Peter Lienau, Lars Ahlberg, Robert Dumas, and John Spencer. All material quoted from the Thurston notebooks came via Stephen McLaughlin, who also helped with Russian/Soviet information. Robert Lundgren kindly provided drawings as well as research from Japanese sources. Help with photographs came from the Boris Lemachko Collection (lemachko@mtu-net.ru) and History on CD-ROM (www.history-on-cdrom.com).

Figure 1. The Turkish *Yavuz* (formerly Germany's *Goeben*).

NIMBLE BOOKS LLC

MISUNDERSTOOD: THE BATTLECRUISER'S PLACE IN HISTORY

❖ "Battlecruisers were never meant to fight against battleships."

❖ "Their large-caliber guns lured admirals into using battlecruisers like battleships, with inevitably disastrous results."

❖ "Designed simply as cruiser-killers, battlecruisers lacked the size of a genuine battleship."

These statements crop up in almost every battlecruiser discussion, which doesn't change the fact that they are all false.

Debate attended each stage of the battlecruiser's existence from conception to demise, and the debate continues decades after its extinction. The issues, unfortunately, became obscured long ago by multiple layers of hindsight, "common knowledge," anachronism, and dueling definitions.

Definitions lie at the root of the problem. What is a battlecruiser? Approached from several perspectives—design lineage, the ship's anticipated role, comparison with other types, or official nomenclature—the question yields multiple valid yet incompatible answers, allowing debaters to hotly disagree while simultaneously being correct. Each of these perspectives deserves consideration, but with a caveat: the definitions freely mutate according to the specifics of place and date.

Starting Point

All this variation heightens the need to start from a fixed reference, such as the starting point of battlecruiser design itself. The battlecruiser began as *an armored cruiser fitted with an all-big-gun armament.* The battlecruiser's design emerged from that of the armored cruiser; it entered the world officially classified as an armored cruiser; and it fulfilled the same role as an armored cruiser. Consequently, an understanding of the battlecruiser must begin with an understanding of the armored cruiser.

Armored cruisers, which featured belt armor in addition to deck protection, appeared as a distinct type in the 1870s when the Russians built *General-Admiral* to threaten British commerce, and the British built *Shannon* to protect commerce from *General-Admiral* and other raiders. But in addition, *Shannon* served as a mini-battleship to challenge foreign ironclads on distant stations. These disparate requirements proved too much for the steam and armor technologies of that time. *Shannon* was a flop.

Figure 2. *General-Admiral* and her sistership *Gertsog-Edinburskii* (seen here) outlived almost all their successors, avoiding the scrapyard until after World War II.

The reliability and logistics of steam propulsion improved soon enough, allowing new ships to forego sailing rig. However, heavy armor remained impractical for designs requiring high speed. This led most fleets to focus on protected cruisers, which carried no thick belts and instead relied on protective decks alone, shielding the vitals below while accepting that shell hits would explode inside the upper hull—hardly an ideal arrangement. Russia persisted with the occasional armored cruiser design and predictably mediocre results. The British felt obligated to match this threat with their own ungratifying set of belted ships but went to the additional expense of purpose-building some second-class battleships (smaller and less brawny than their first-class cousins, but also faster) to serve as station ships and cruiser-killers,[1] while also building a multitude of protected cruisers to bear the main burden of commerce protection.

As the century neared its end, advances in metallurgy created new armor that, even in relatively thin plates, could defeat heavy shells. Nickel steel, then Harvey armor, then Krupp cemented armor—this lightweight protection meant that even a fast ship could approach battleship-grade protection, which was good news since cruisers sometimes approached battleship-grade size and price tags. (In 1897, Britain com-

---

[1] The term "cruiser-killer" had no significant currency at the time, but "cruiser-destroyer" made its way into British ink no later than 1885—coincidentally, just as the world's navies began building a new type known as the "destroyer" (i.e., "torpedo boat destroyer"). Confusion ensued.

pleted the 11,690-ton second-class battleship *Renown*, the 14,700-ton protected cruiser *Powerful*, and the 14,980-ton first-class battleship *Jupiter*.) In fact it was this period that saw the first reference to battlecruisers, no later than 1893. In that year, a paper presented to British designers argued that the "size and offensive powers" of some cruisers would "justify attaching the name of battle-cruisers" to them. Though it would take the term nearly twenty years to cement its now-familiar meaning, the 19th Century author had no trouble discussing the brawny cruiser alongside the "battle-ship of less speed" or theorizing that "offensive power and speed may be developed in future battleships at the expense of armoured protection."[2]

The Japanese were among the first to grasp this new cruiser potential. Having bought only one armored cruiser previously, they commissioned six from 1899 to 1901, the result of their "6-6 Fleet" plan which envisioned these new cruisers as half the fleet's battle line. At the Battle of Tsushima, Japan not only used armored cruisers in the line of battle, but had great success with them.

This facet of the Japanese victory surprised no one because the armored cruiser was an accepted citizen of battle lines all around the world, and no strict distinction divided the armored cruisers from battleships. Britain's Admiral John Fisher regarded the large armored cruiser as "a swift Battleship in disguise." The ambiguity was old news in America, where the first armored cruiser, *Maine*, began construction in 1888 only to be re-rated a second-class battleship before completion. The subsequent *New York* managed to remain an armored cruiser, but the Secretary of the Navy felt that the ship's "chances … are not to be despised should she be driven to a momentary encounter with a battleship."[3] American writers eagerly heralded *New York* as a "cruiser destroyer," and in 1902 the esteemed naval architect William Hovgaard found the term suitable for the upcoming *Tennessee* class.[4] Personnel drafting its plans were cautioned about loose lips, lest Congress hear that funds for the fleet's new "cruisers" had in fact gone to "fast battleships." The use of state names for these ships apparently aroused no suspicion.

---

[2] Long, Samuel. "On the Present Position of Cruisers in Naval Warfare." *Transactions of the Institute of Naval Architects*, Vol. 34, 1893, pp. 3, 5. A truly curious reference appears in an 1882 report to the United States Congress (Report No. 653, "Construction of Vessels of War for the Navy") which includes a survey of foreign armored ships. In the Austrian listing, several ships receive the description "line-of-battle cruiser." The text offers no clue as to the intended meaning of this phrase, or its origins. It certainly did not come from the Austrians, who rated the ships as frigates and casemate ships— unremarkable terminology for an unremarkable set of ships.

[3] Friedman, Norman. *U.S. Cruisers*. Naval Institute Press, 1984, p. 35.

[4] *Transactions of the Society of Naval Architects and Marine Engineers*, Vol. 10, 1902, p. 286. Also around this time, official Commonwealth proposals began to mention a "cruiser-destroyer" (apparently a 3,000-ton scout with no particular aptitude for cruising or destroying) which politicians and the press mistook for a large, cruiser-like destroyer. The proposals died, but the term lasted some years as an option when reporters didn't know how else to label a ship. The original definition endured at least to 1918 when it appeared in reports on French design studies for a commerce raider capable of fighting a battleship. By then, a spirit of one-upmanship had prompted a U.S. coast defense officer to tag a British ship (probably *Hood*) as not only a "battle-cruiser-destroyer" but a "superdreadnaught-destroyer."

1289 – U. S. ARMORED CRUISER "PENNSYLVANIA." 800 OFFICERS AND MEN.
LENGTH 502 FEET. MAIN BATTERY 18 GUNS.

Figure 3. From 1905 to 1908, the Americans commissioned twenty-three ships named after states—thirteen battleships and ten armored cruisers.

Similar confusion applied outside the English-speaking world. The Italians never had a separate rating for their armored cruisers but simply clumped their *Pisa* and *San Giorgio* classes together with the most recent battleships as *navi da battaglia di 1ᵃ classe*. The French began to see the armored cruiser as, in the words of theorist Admiral François-Ernest Fournier, a ship "good at doing everything." Fournier had such faith in his *Dupuy de Lôme* of 1895 that he considered her capable of confronting a battleship, in addition to her other duties. The Russians showed the spectrum of priorities in their two *Ryuriks*; the *Ryurik* of 1895 carried more coal for long raiding cruises while the *Ryurik* of 1908, Russia's final armored cruiser, sacrificed some fuel but carried such heavy weaponry that her secondary battery doubled the older ship's main battery[5]—battle-line brawn had become paramount.

Now and Then

An observer today, looking back through a hundred years of naval development, might have trouble seeing a justification for the use of cruisers against battleships. But in the context of naval warfare and weaponry of that era—not of World War I or World War II or any other period—the picture is clear.

While a battleship in World War II might displace three times the tonnage of a heavy cruiser, and thus could steamroll any cruiser in its path, this did not parallel the naval realities of forty years earlier, before the Washington Treaty limits at 10,000 tons and 8-inch guns imposed alien and arbitrary constraints on what a cruiser could

---

[5] The elder ship carried four 8-inch guns; the newer, eight 8-inch guns…plus four 10-inch guns.

be. Little relationship exists between armored cruisers and the later heavy cruisers. Many armored cruisers ranked as capital ships—both *Ryuriks*, at the time of commissioning, became the largest units in the Russian fleet—a status never dreamed of for a heavy cruiser. Yet the superficial resemblances create an illusory connection. For example, *Pennsylvania* of 1905 and *Pittsburgh* of 1944 both carried 8-inch guns on a design displacement near 15,000 tons. But more important than the similarity, the contrast leaps out: the largest US battleship serving in 1905 displaced 13,000 tons, compared to the 54,000-ton monsters of 1944.[6]

Likewise, the battle ranges and the advanced weaponry of 1940s battleships made them supreme in a gun fight; but at the close quarters of turn-of-the-century combat, the 8-inch gun of an armored cruiser could nearly match the accurate trajectory of a battleship's 12-inch gun. And while the larger shell was indisputably more destructive, the heavy guns fired slowly, allowing the quicker guns to compensate for the lesser effect of individual hits. Furthermore, shell design had not yet advanced to match the advances in armor quality, so that even an armored cruiser had a reasonable hope of resisting the largest shells. The entire Russo-Japanese War produced only a handful of penetrations of 6-inch armor plates.

Few cruiser advocates took these factors alone to indicate equality with battleships. The cruiser had an additional card to play, its greater speed, which meant it didn't have to square off with a battleship and trade broadsides. Cruisers could outmaneuver their battleship enemies and find positions of tactical superiority to offset their lesser brawn, just as the faster Japanese fleet was able to cross the Russian "T" at Tsushima. Or a cruiser could dash in and engage a battleship already under battleship fire. Cruisers could harry the rear of a withdrawing fleet or pounce on wounded ships.

This is exactly how the largest fleet, the Royal Navy, anticipated using its armored cruisers in a fleet engagement. Having gone through the 1890s without commissioning an armored cruiser—though private yards built export models for Japan and others—the British returned to the type with great enthusiasm: the *Cressy, Drake, Monmouth, Devonshire, Duke of Edinburgh, Warrior,* and *Minotaur* classes totaling thirty-five ships all laid down by 1905, giving Britain the most powerful set of armored cruisers. These ships would be split among various duties as commerce protectors, fleet scouts, and the fast wing of the battle line.

However, the British themselves were about to change the world of the armored cruiser. Admiral Fisher held these ships in high regard. He went as far as to suggest phasing out the Royal Navy's battleships altogether in favor of an enlarged armored cruiser fleet—a proposal that failed, but he continued with other ideas, subtler but also far-reaching. He advocated uniform main batteries for armored cruisers, and he grasped the newly emerging benefits of large-caliber guns. The invention of advanced gunnery controls started the world's navies into planning battles at greater ranges, ranges which would degrade the hit rate and striking energy of 8-inch weaponry more rapidly than those of 12-inch guns. And the newest 12-inch guns were no longer the

---

[6] The head of the Bureau of Equipment remarked that *Pennsylvania* "should be ready to fight almost anything, even a battleship." No sane person ever suggested *Pittsburgh* might challenge *Yamato*.

slow, clumsy things of just a few years earlier. The factors that led to the dreadnought battleship also dictated the logic of creating a dreadnought cruiser.

Advent of the Battlecruiser

As stated previously, the battlecruiser was an armored cruiser with all-big-gun weaponry. The Royal Navy officially labeled the first battlecruisers, the *Invincible* class, as armored cruisers until adopting the "battle cruiser" rating in 1911,[7] more than three years after the ships started into service. In the meantime, any number of unofficial terms sprang up: cruiser-battleship, battleship-cruiser, dreadnought-cruiser, and so forth—none of them as dramatic (that is, marketable) as "battle cruiser." The change in nomenclature tends to obscure the fact that the battlecruiser had the same roles as the armored cruiser; the switch to all big guns, and to turbine engines, simply improved the cruiser's ability to fulfill its mission.

Unfortunately, the fact that Fisher actively concealed his reasoning makes it impossible to sort out all the concepts in the battlecruiser's gestation. And while Fisher excelled as an idea generator, it's unclear to what degree his ideas ever stabilized into a coherent whole. Nevertheless, some factors appear certain. First, Fisher believed that the battlecruiser could use its speed to achieve and maintain a position of tactical superiority, providing a decisive advantage even against nominally more powerful battleships. Second, Fisher expected the battlecruiser to eclipse the battleship and become the standard capital ship.[8] Yet things did not develop as he anticipated.

Britain's looming rival, Imperial Germany, copied the battlecruiser concept and ended Fisher's hope for decisive advantage. To make matters worse, Britain fell behind Germany in developing armor-piercing shells. The old norms of cruiser protection no longer sufficed, and Germany's battlecruisers had armor more in keeping with battleship standards. Compounded with the hazard of volatile British cordite, this led directly to the Royal Navy's battlecruiser disaster at Jutland. The Jutland experience doesn't justify condemnation of the battlecruiser as a type—the German ships performed creditably enough—but it underscored underscores the type's vulnerability to technological missteps.

Ironically, Jutland has become the "proof" of several misconceptions that in reality it refutes. Despite statements to the contrary, no Jutland battlecruiser fell victim to battleships. And the idea that battlecruisers lacked battleship tonnage runs aground on the fact that Britain's largest Jutland ship was the battlecruiser *Tiger*, and Germany's was the battlecruiser *Lützow*. Since turn-of-the-century cruisers often reached battleship size, it is no surprise that by 1910 battlecruiser designs ran larger than corresponding battleship designs, as seen in both the German and the British navies.

---

[7] Admiralty Weekly Order No. 351 of 24 November 1911.

[8] Many authors have analyzed Fisher's thinking, but the claims in this passage derive mostly from three works. Roberts, John. *Battlecruisers*. Chatham Publishing, 1999, p. 25. Brooks, John. *Dreadnought Gunnery and the Battle of Jutland*. Routledge, 2005, pp. 1-2. Sumida, Jon Tetsuro. "British Capital Ship Design and Fire Control in the *Dreadnought* Era: Sir John Fisher, Arthur Hungerford Pollen, and the Battle Cruiser." *The Journal of Modern History*, Vol. 51, No. 2, June 1979, pp. 207-210.

Figure 4. The *Invincible*-class "armoured cruiser" *Inflexible*.

Figure 5. Germany's first battlecruiser, *Von der Tann*, established that Britain could not assume qualitative superiority.

Table 1. Battleship and battlecruiser sizes compared as of 1909.

Class	Type	First unit laid down	Tonnage
Moltke	German battlecruiser	January 1909	22,616
Helgoland	German battleship	October 1908	22,448
Lion	British battlecruiser	November 1909	26,350
Orion	British battleship	November 1909	21,922

The Fast Battleship

In the wake of Jutland, the situation for large cruisers changed again, and again the British spurred the process. They completed their battlecruiser *Hood* in 1920, simultaneously commissioning the world's largest warship and tying the battlecruiser debate into a Gordian knot. *Hood* had the speed of a battlecruiser and the armor of a battleship.

By official RN rating, *Hood* was a "battle cruiser," but British thinking had clearly shifted. A 1935 Admiralty document says, "Following the principle worked to in the case of the HOOD, a battle cruiser's protection should be the same as that of a battleship."[9] This was no British aberration. In 1934, a United States Navy (USN) ship designer informed his colleagues that the "protective system of the battle cruiser should be comparable in efficiency ... to that of the battleship."[10] The word *battlecruiser* no longer had its original meaning.

Unfortunately, with *Hood*'s destruction in 1941 routinely dismissed as just another battlecruiser blowing up, the change in battlecruiser concept that she represented goes unnoticed. In fact, analysis of the Denmark Strait battle shows that *Hood* did not suffer for having a "battlecruiser" armor scheme—she was arguably the best-protected ship in the Royal Navy at the time of her completion—but she suffered instead for having a World War I armor scheme in World War II. Any unmodernized battleship might have succumbed to a similar hit. In fact, *Hood* herself demonstrated the potential of 15-inch gunnery against an unmodernized battleship when she shelled *Bretagne* at Mers el Kebir and caused her to explode. This leads to a historical curiosity—*Hood* was the only battlecruiser ever sunk by a battleship, and *Hood* was the only battlecruiser ever to sink a battleship. The battleship-versus-battlecruiser score is a tie.

But once again, definitions and official terminology muddle the issue, as it appears that the Guadalcanal Campaign included the destruction of a battlecruiser (*Kirishima*) by a pair of battleships (*Washington* and *South Dakota*). However, the Japanese

---

[9] ADM 1/9387: Capital Ships—Protection.

[10] Rossell, H.E. "The Battle Cruiser." *Transactions of the Society of Naval Architects and Marine Engineers*, Vol. 42, 1934, p. 269.

navy had discontinued its battlecruiser rating (*junyô-senkan*, literally "cruiser-battleship") in 1931 when the *Kongos* underwent their first modernization, gaining armor but sacrificing speed; from that time, *Kirishima* and her sisters officially became battleships with the same rating as all other Japanese battleships (*senkan*). Whether or not the armor upgrades or the speed loss justified this re-rating is a matter of opinion, which reflects Fisher's observation that categorizing capital ships was like defining the instant when a kitten became a cat. And while many would debate *Kirishima*'s status, most neglect to question whether or not *Washington* and *South Dakota* deserved to be called battleships.

Capital ship design and nomenclature did not stand still after World War I. Only one pure battleship project reached completion after the Washington Treaty, the *Nelson* class (which, ironically enough, developed from a battlecruiser design that had its armor thinned and the speed greatly reduced). As for subsequent battlecruisers, no completed capital ships show the same favoritism of speed over armor, and yet the slowest post-*Nelson* battleships had more speed than the fastest World War I battleship.

The battleship had undergone a fundamental change in speed standards. The old *California* and the new *North Carolina* provide an instructive example. As modernized, the old ship had a level of armor protection comparable to the new ship's, and *North Carolina* was originally intended to carry twelve 14-inch guns as *California* did. The salient difference lay in the 7-knot speed increase, an observation so obvious that the terms "modern battleship" and "fast battleship" became synonymous.

In 1937, *The New York Times* observed, "Evidently the old distinction between battleships and battle cruisers has lost its validity when we behold European Powers combining the high speed of the battle cruiser with the adequate armor and long-range hitting power of the battleship." The modern battleship was a hybrid: half battleship and half battlecruiser.

A Battleship by Any Other Name

Definitions always present a moving target. Official nomenclature does its duty as a fixed reference, but as an indicator of ship characteristics, it has dubious value. A ship's rating might reveal some tactical reality or might conceal it, as the Japanese would prove with their *Kongos*. Politics could distort the situation, as with the *Tennessee* class "cruisers" mentioned above or in the famous case of the German "pocket battleships." Language itself could change; in the 1930s, the Germans adopted the term *Schlachtschiff* (battleship) in preference to the older *Linienschiff* which in common usage had come to mean a passenger liner rather than a ship-of-the-battle-line. Each navy formulated its own practice for its own reasons.

Britain. Having bent the definition of battlecruiser by applying it to *Hood*, the Royal Navy then applied it to all the world's fast battleships such as *Dunkerque* and *Scharnhorst*. Documents in the early phase of the new *King George V* project include the battlecruiser term, and Britain's final battleship *Vanguard* gestated as a "fully armoured battlecruiser" (a curious term but no more oxymoronic than "fast battleship"). The realization in the 1930s that no navy would again dare to build a slow capital ship caused the Admiralty to revamp its terminology, generalizing the "battleship" term and thus sparing itself the discomfort of linking its modern ships to the Jutland victims.

Figure 6. The *King George V* design, a "battlecruiser" in the *Hood* tradition. (History on CD-ROM)

France. Naval records show a hopeless maze of categories that often changed and occasionally overlapped. For armored cruisers, *croiseur cuirassé* proved most popular, with some variation of *cuirassé* for battleships. The standard label for foreign battle-cruisers, *croiseur de bataille,* had no domestic relevance as the French never built such a ship themselves, although they came close. The Naval Law of 1912 provided for an expansion of the fleet, including a set of fleet scouts (*éclaireurs d'escadre*) and station ships (*bâtiments pour divisions lointaines*). The precise nature of these ships remained undefined, and world events prompted a spirit of escalation that drove proposals to battleship size. The *croiseur de bataille* term surfaced, along with *cuirassé-croiseur*, *croiseur de combat*, and *grand éclaireur d'escadre*. But none of these tags found a home as the war halted all development. When work resumed after the Washington Treaty, *croiseur de bataille* reappeared in company with *croiseur protégé* (a term the French hadn't used in ordering their old protected cruisers, but did use for these capital ships and simultaneously for treaty cruisers). Ultimately a *croiseur de combat* plan developed into the *Dunkerque*, but by the time she became official, she was a battleship—*bâtiment de ligne*, a term salvaged from the Age of Sail and distinct from the inclusive *navire de ligne* (capital ship) in the French text of the Washington Treaty. Following *Dunkerque*, mighty *Richelieu* had the same rating.

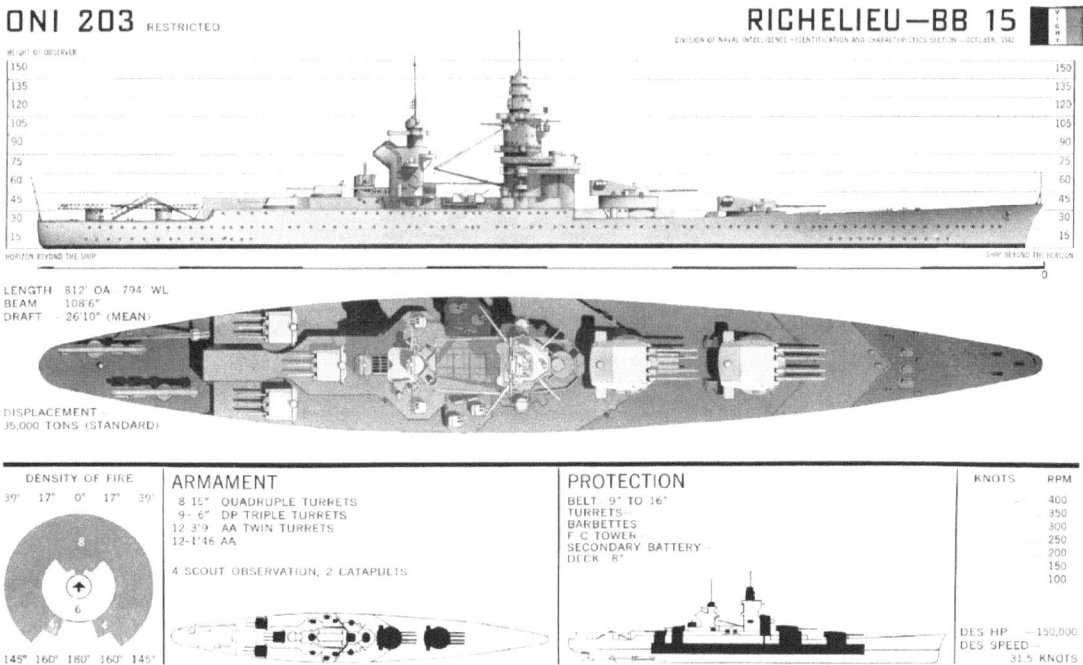

Figure 7. American intelligence understated *Richelieu*'s speed. She achieved her designed 32 knots on trials and momentarily topped 32.5 knots, making her faster than any World War I battlecruiser. (History on CD-ROM)

Italy. In contrast, the *Regia Marina* never wavered from labeling all capital ships as battleships, though they varied between the more general *navi da battaglia* (warships) and the specific *corazzati* (battleships). At their most extravagant, they added a gradation (1st class, 2nd class, etc.) or an adjective (*corazzate rapide* for the *Caracciolo* design).

Germany. The cunning set of naval laws, engineered by Tirpitz, dictated a strict division between cruisers and battleships. Thus, as armored cruisers phased into battlecruisers, the term *Großer Kreuzer* (large cruiser) could not change. This rigid system had an ulterior purpose, to conceal the fact that in 1918 the navy would effectively shrug off political oversight of its fleet composition. As 1918 drew near, the "GK" prefix of cruiser design proposals drifted from meaning *Großer Kreuzer* and settled instead on *Großkampfschiff* (large fighting ship), with some designs mounting the same main battery as proposals in the "L" line of battleship designs (*Linienschiffes*). At the same time, the "L" proposals showed a sudden boost in speed. This convergence of the two lines into an *Einheitsschiff*, a unified design of great armor and speed, might have faltered for lack of funds, but instead Germany's defeat and the Versailles Treaty imposed a harsher stop. The treaty allowed for "armored ships" (a term copied from the official rating for coast-defense battleships in various northern European navies), but the Germans turned this definition on its head and instead built commerce raiders (which they eventually re-rated as heavy cruisers). Nazi-era programs assigned the new and stirringly Wagnerian *Schlachtschiffe* designation to the *Scharnhorst* and *Bismarck* classes. Only at the very end did Germany initiate a *Schlachtkreuzer* project; the "OPQ" class, which earned the nickname *Ohne Panzer Quatsch* (Without Armor Nonsense), never began construction.

Figure 8. The battleship *Gneisenau* carried guns weaker than a World War I battlecruiser's.

Austria-Hungary. Given the Austrians' naval penny-pinching, their fleet had little need to wrangle with cruiser categories. An armored cruiser was simply an "armored cruiser" (*Panzerkreuzer*).[11] *Invincible*'s launch caused minimal ripples—"*Großer Panzerkreuzer*" appeared in discussions—but *Goeben*'s race to Turkey generated excitement. Admirals spoke of *Gefechtskreuzer* (combat cruisers). No construction took place, but designers produced preliminary studies, making references to *Schlachtkreuzer*.

---

[11] German served as the official language for the Austro-Hungarian Navy.

Russia. The earliest Russian battlecruisers, the *Izmail*s, began under the heading of "armored cruisers" (*bronenosnye kreisera*) but became "cruisers of the line" (*lineinye kreisera*) before their construction dragged to a halt. When the Soviets resurrected dreadnought construction, they distinguished *Sovetskii Soyuz*, their thickly protected battleship (*lineinyi korabl'*), from *Kronshtadt*, their somewhat protected battlecruiser (literally "heavy cruiser," *tyazhyolyi kreiser*).

United States. The Americans tagged all their dreadnoughts as battleships except for the incomplete *Lexington*-class "battle cruisers" and the *Alaska* class "large cruisers." Much debate has arisen over *Alaska*'s unique rating—unique to the USN, at least, though perfectly familiar to the Germans. The choice not to repeat the battlecruiser rating indicates that the leadership saw *Alaska* as something different, and rightly so; commerce protection was the driving force behind the project, while *Lexington* had specialized as a heavy scout.[12] In a fleet engagement, *Alaska* would not form up with the battleships but would act as a screen for them, and since her design lineage extended back to the light cruisers of the *Pensacola* class, "large cruiser" may be appropriate.[13] For those alarmed by the similarity to Britain's "large light cruiser" rating, *Alaska*'s balanced design clearly distinguishes her from the *Courageous* class.

Figure 9. Few students of naval history would dare call *Alaska* a battleship.

Japan. Kongo hatched from proposals pre-dating *Invincible*, so her earliest official label, *ittô junyôkan* (first-class cruiser), grouped her with Japan's other armored cruisers; her individual construction order actually said *sôkô junyôkan* (armored cruiser). Inspired by the British, the Japanese adopted "battlecruiser" in 1912 but, having dropped it in 1931, never revived it even though *Kongo*'s second modernization greatly boosted her speed to adapt her for the un-battleship-like task of supporting torpedo attacks. Yet when formulating a new design for this same role, the Japanese catego-

---

[12] Early drafts of the design called *Lexington* a "battle scout."

[13] *Alaska* took form under the heading of "heavy cruiser." In design terms, a heavy cruiser is actually a type of light cruiser.

rized the ship as a "Super-A cruiser" (*chô kô junyôkan*—that is, a super heavy cruiser) and tagged it with the traditional "B" prefix of battlecruiser proposals (Design B-65).

Netherlands. The Dutch began investigating a small design of their own in the 1930s. They initially considered building a *Dunkerque* derivative, but the lack of French cooperation sent them to the Germans who helped them develop their Project 1047 with a look reminiscent of *Scharnhorst's*. German records referred to the *Holland-Schlachtschiffe*, but the Dutch, aware that modern designs merged battleship and battlecruiser qualities, opted for a *slagkruiser* rating to emphasize that these ships could never directly challenge the larger, more numerous, and better-supported battleships of rival Japan.

The New "Battlecruisers"

This draws attention to yet another complication. Like *Alaska* and B-65, the first modern battleships had modest size—*Dunkerque* and *Scharnhorst*, both described as near 26,000 tons. They came to public attention during the time when the Royal Navy regarded any fast capital ship as a battlecruiser. The 1937 edition of Britain's official *Fleets* guide reclassified *Dunkerque* and *Scharnhorst*, changing them from their native rating as battleships to battlecruisers. Later, designs like *Bismarck*, *King George V*, and *Littorio* approached the same speed standard, but what distinguished them from *Dunkerque* and *Scharnhorst* was their greater size *plus* the fact that the Royal Navy had reverted to calling them battleships. The inferred connection between size and the battleship rating gave rise to yet another definition of the battlecruiser, perhaps the most prevalent now and the most misleading—that of a small, weak battleship.

Several navies developed designs below the established treaty norm of 35,000 tons, and English-language sources have categorized them all as battlecruisers. In fact, within the greater context of capital ship design, many of these ships might qualify as second-class battleships (faster, weaker, and smaller) rather than as battlecruisers (faster, weaker, and larger). Design B-65 had gunpower and armor like a scaled-down *Yamato's* but with high speed and torpedoes more typical of a cruiser. *Alaska* too blended cruiser and battleship characteristics, like her single rudder and her inclined belt. This should cause no confusion. It merely confirms the ships as hybrids, something they share with the full-sized designs. Agonizing over the proper battleship/battlecruiser label makes as much sense as arguing whether a mule is a horse or a donkey.

Conclusion

Given the great breadth of designs, doctrines, and terms associated with the battlecruiser, any discussion imposing rigid definitions will tend to deepen the ruts of prevailing misconception. The battlecruiser represented a multi-purpose platform, and each navy had its own ideas about customizing the concept to suit its particular needs. These ideas changed over time, sometimes dramatically. The consequently fluid nature of terminology means that even the most general assertion—for example, that battlecruisers had less armor than battleships—requires qualification. Generalities can help in laying out the principles for battleship-battlecruiser comparison, but the most fruitful discussions require an appreciation of each design. Thus the strict division of capital ships into two categories fails to properly model what was in reality a spectrum of blends of protection, firepower, size, and mobility. While it would go too far to call labels meaningless, the intense laboring after labels hinders rather than helps. Once the battlecruiser debate escapes the tyranny of definitions, then the historical record can emerge in proper focus.

THE FIRST BATTLECRUISER

The battlecruiser, in adopting both a uniform main battery and battleship-caliber guns, represents an even greater revolution than the dreadnought battleship. The *Invincible* class stands as the first to embody these changes, but other claims make a challenge.

Addressing an assembly of naval designers in Kobe in 1914, Rear Admiral Motoki Kondo stated, "The name 'battle-cruiser' is of a comparatively recent date, and ships forming this class are supposed to combine the qualities of battleships and cruisers. I think our Navy ought to have the credit for the creation of this class." He specifically cited the *Asamas*, oldest of the armored cruisers in the Tsushima battle line, as the "pioneers" of the battlecruiser type. Kondo's understandable pride in the record of these ships cannot negate the fact that the *Asama* design (actually a British product) introduced nothing revolutionary to the international set of armored cruisers that preceded it, such as Italy's *Garibaldi*.[14] In fact, *Asama* resulted from a refinement of a previous British design, Chile's *O'Higgins*.

❖ *O'Higgins* (1898): 8,500 tons, 7-inch belt armor, four 8-inch and ten 6-inch guns, 21.6 knots

❖ *Asama* (1899): 9,700 tons, 7-inch belt armor, four 8-inch and fourteen 6-inch guns, 21.5 knots

---

[14] Italy pioneered the armored cruiser as a battle-line combatant, and *Garibaldi* played a key role in selling the British on the idea. When the *Garibaldi* design hit the export market, Japan bought two units in time to serve alongside *Asama* at Tsushima. Admiral Kondo's enthusiasm belonged more properly with them.

Figure 10. *Asama* mounted four 8-inch guns more efficiently than her Chilean forebear, in twin centerline turrets.

Asama certainly improved over earlier ships, sometimes in ways not apparent in bare statistics; but likewise did subsequent ships surpass *Asama*. A fine ship, but not revolutionary, she represented just one of many evolutionary steps in cruiser development.

Perhaps a better claim belongs to another Japanese cruiser, *Tsukuba*, a design that did at least include one major advance, its four battleship-caliber guns.[15] The Japanese went as far as re-rating *Tsukuba* as a battlecruiser after the British adopted the term, but the chief result of this measure was to showcase *Tsukuba*'s inferiority to *Invincible*, a true battlecruiser with eight big guns and 25 knots. Even if historians lower the bar to accept *Tsukuba* as a battlecruiser, it remains difficult to support her claim of revolutionary capability when a battleship completed in Italy three years earlier seems nearly her equal.

- ❖ *Regina Margherita* (1904): 13,215 tons, 6-inch[16] belt armor, four 12-inch and four 8-inch and twelve 6-inch guns, 20.3 knots

- ❖ *Tsukuba* (1907): 13,750 tons, 7-inch belt armor, four 12-inch and twelve 6-inch guns, 20.5 knots

Again, statistics tell only part of the story, but it would require some creativity to find a battlecruiser definition that allowed *Tsukuba* a claim as the first.

For those approaching the subject from the other direction, a uniform main battery might stake a claim for Germany's *Blücher*, even if the guns were 8.2-inch and indisputably too small to rate as battleship-caliber. In France, *Edgar Quinet* commissioned after *Blücher* but began construction before, mounting a uniform 7.6-inch battery. However, both the British and the Americans had already completed armored cruisers with uniform 6-inch batteries.

The obvious inferiority of these cruiser-caliber guns effectively cancels any battlecruiser pretensions. It was the battleship-caliber weaponry that drove the Dreadnought Revolution, leaving *Invincible* secure as the first battlecruiser.

---

[15] Of course, one could argue that 10-inch guns qualified as battleship-caliber, allowing candidates like *Tennessee* and *Ryurik*—but no one would listen.

[16] Regarding plate thickness only, 1 inch = 24.9mm (except for American ships).

HMS COURAGEOUS—WHAT THE HECK?

Mysteries often diminish as time casts new light into history's dim corners. But then, some things just get darker and darker.

Courageous, Glorious, and *Furious* have beset observers with a barrage of perplexities regarding their design, their mission, even their nomenclature. (The nicknames Outrageous, Curious, and Spurious are hardly the least frustrated titles flung their way.)

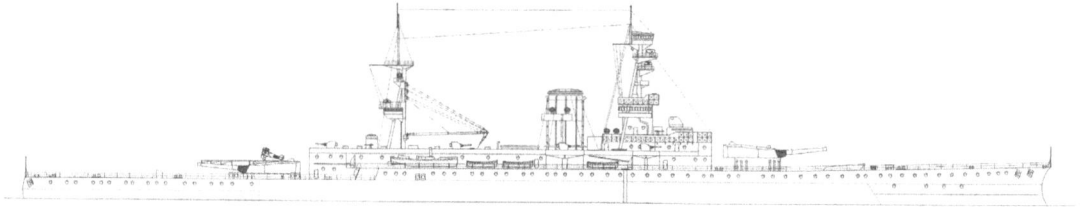

Figure 11. HMS *Courageous* (Robert Lundgren)

The questions begin with the man behind the project, Admiral John Fisher. Previously, as the key player in the Dreadnought Revolution, he built on the advantages of a uniform main battery and created ships with broadsides of eight guns rather than the four of pre-dreadnoughts. However, it may be that he never understood the gunnery significance of an eight-gun broadside; ten years later, his *Courageous* regressed to four guns (two 15-inch twin turrets). When these numerically challenged weapons had their solitary opportunity to fire at enemy ships, they did more harm than good.[17] Similarly, the secondary battery harked back to the days when 4-inch guns with their 31-lb shells seemed adequate against smaller targets like destroyers, though the rest of the world had progressed to guns of 5-6 inches firing shells of 50-100 lbs.[18]

In all this, *Furious* found herself singled out for compounded caricature, assigned to carry a main battery of two single turrets, 18-inchers, only one of which she ever received.[19] And while she had the good fortune to receive a realistic secondary battery of 5.5-inch guns, the rearmament accomplished little except to make a bigger freak of her, as she never went into combat with any of these weapons.

The protection scheme made no more sense than the weaponry. At 19,000 tons, *Courageous* had 3-inch belt armor, just like the 4000-ton "C"-class light cruisers entering service at the time.[20] The 3-inch figure actually overstates the level of protection since the belt didn't comprise single-thickness armor-grade steel as one might expect in a battlecruiser belt—rather, two layers of high-tensile (HT) steel, 2-inch atop 1-inch. These factors degraded the belt's shell resistance by more than 15% from its

---

[17] One inconsequential hit on the enemy versus self-damage via blast and a premature shellburst.

[18] Admittedly, Spain was still working on *España*'s long-delayed sistership, laid down years before, with 4-inch secondaries.

[19] The forward part of the ship remained clear as a platform for aviation trials.

[20] The "C" class carried 6-inch guns with a shell weighing 5% as much as a 15-inch shell.

nominal 3-inch value. Of course, for a ship with 15-inch guns, the difference between a 3-inch and a 2.5-inch belt seems inconsequential.

In some ways, fortunately, *Courageous* rose above the standards of a normal light cruiser. Her full belt thickness covered the magazines, where "C" had only 2-inch HT steel. Her citadel had deck protection (notwithstanding the fact that none of it exceeded 1-inch until Jutland inspired some reinforcement). More dramatically, the main battery had real armor—7-inch barbettes and 9-inch turret faceplates—to go with the 10-inch conning tower. Conceivably, a ship might have a role necessitating such disproportionate armor, if only some clues existed to the role intended for *Courageous*.

Usually a ship's official rating gives an indication, but in this case, it indicates nothing but confusion. The Royal Navy categorized *Courageous* and her sisters as "first class cruisers"—a term not used since the large protected cruisers of the 19th Century. And yet, there one can find a design almost analogous to *Courageous*. The *Powerful* class[21] of 1895 nearly doubled the tonnage of the preceding *Edgar* class simply to boost her mobility. This did not make the ships valuable. *Conway's* calls the *Powerfuls* "white elephants as they required a very large crew, were costly to operate and did not fulfill any true requirement of the Navy."

Indeed, "white elephant" may be the most popular label for the *Courageous* class, but decades of commentary have produced options aplenty: the straightforward fun of "Fisher's Follies," the more metaphoric "An Old Man's Children," or "Something very special in the way of madness." Perhaps "Weird Sisters" lends a suitably classical air. More formal attempts resulted in the oxymorons "light battlecruisers" and "large light cruisers" which do good service in acknowledging the design's self-contradictions and hanging a fig leaf on its lack of purpose. An official wartime roster classed the ships as a "Special Type" of battlecruiser, confirming the British mastery of understatement.

Since the Ship's Covers for the *Courageous* class include nothing prior to formulation of their design requirements, the only clues to the original concept lie in letters and discussions; Fisher's involvement casts them all in a dubious light. His famed Baltic Plan called for the Royal Navy to press eastward in support for Russian operations there. The *Courageous* hull had limited draft that suited her to Baltic waters. Fisher sent a memo to Britain's design chief so they could get their stories straight while arguing for the design's approval. "We must stick to it that draught of water will not exceed 22½ feet, this is vital for Baltic work. It's on the Baltic undertaking that he will carry them through in the Cabinet." The Baltic Plan itself, however, was just another Fisher bluff; the secretary of Britain's war cabinet expressed his view that "the whole plan was a chimera from the very beginning" but saw its roots in actual plans for assaulting German positions along the Channel and North Sea coasts. Such operations gave rise to specialized designs such as monitors—i.e., shallow-draft vessels carrying battleship-caliber guns.

---

[21] The *Powerful* design carried a main battery of two 9.2-inch single turrets backed by 6-inch guns after progressing from specifications for a uniform battery of 6-inchers.

Some of Fisher's comments do foster the queasy thought that he saw battlecruisers as 30-knot monitors; he even fantasized a 20-inch version whose shells would start the German Army "fleeing for its life from Pomerania to Berlin." He even explained the half-sized main battery: "The 'Furious' (and all her breed) were not built for salvoes! They were built for Berlin...."[22] Yet thoroughbred cruisers had little in common with sturdy monitors that struggled to reach ten knots but had genuinely shallow draft (about 10 feet). Both types mounted 15-inch and 18-inch guns, but while monitors actually wielded them in shore bombardment, *Courageous* and her sisters never indulged in such things. In fact, at no time in their design or service did their ammunition loadout call for the high-explosive shells used in bombardment duty.

Figure 12. *Furious* herself appears confused, with her single 18-inch gun aft and a flight deck forward.

Without a viable Baltic Plan or monitor connection, *Courageous*'s shallow draft needs another explanation. Hull studies at the time indicated that shallow draft offered a way to limit underwater damage, so this one feature of the design may actually originate in common sense.

Common sense, though, can't explain the design as a whole. Another of Fisher's tales, while less well known, seems more convincing than the Baltic one he relied on. Noting an incompatibility between the fleet's battlecruisers and the light cruisers operating with them, he wrote, "The present small cruisers get their speed knocked down at once to 15 knots in heavy weather so will be no use to accompany and scout for the BCs & may fall prey to the enemy's BCs if caught by them scouting in heavy weather."[23] This would cast *Courageous* as a light cruiser enlarged for increased mobil-

---

[22] Roberts, *Battlecruisers*, p 51.

[23] *Ibid*. Also McBride, Keith. "The Weird Sisters," *Warship 1990*, p 104.

ity, but like so many things that Fisher said, it may not represent any genuine conviction. History certainly established the design as a failure versus light cruisers (as Fisher himself anticipated with his comment on salvo fire), and no one needs history to establish the design's prospects versus a battlecruiser.

Had designers tailored a ship to this mission, they might have managed it on only half the tonnage of a *Courageous*. In fact, the British built precisely such a design, the *Hawkins* class, which showed numerous commonalities with *Courageous*. Though not specialized for fleet operations, *Hawkins* mounted weapons and armor superior to a "C's" and possessed excellent sea-keeping so she could overtake commerce-raiding light cruisers in any conditions.[24] This was also a role that Fisher sporadically attempted to pin on *Courageous*, saying she could operate "against any of the enemy cruisers that might get out into the open seas and attack merchant ships."[25] All in all, it seems that Fisher was willing to throw anything against the wall until something stuck, which still leaves the question, What was his actual goal?

The search for a rationale within the *Courageous* design itself assumes the existence of such a rationale. Matching a 7-inch barbette with a 3-inch belt, putting battleship guns on a ship armored against light-cruiser shells, providing high speed to a ship with no place to go—the possibility exists that the decision was irrational, a monster slipping through the disconnect between an admiral's fantasy and the realities of naval combat.

Or perhaps combat was a secondary concern. Shortly after the outbreak of the Great War, Fisher became First Sea Lord and had to reconcile the government's refusal to fund battlecruisers with his own devotion to the type. Seizing on the opportunity presented by two suspended "R" class battleships, he managed to get them recast as the battlecruisers *Renown* and *Repulse*, armed with previously ordered 15-inch twin turrets.[26] More turrets remained available, but no more vacant capital ship orders. Light cruisers, though, remained an option, and Fisher again found a way to put big guns on a fast hull, entirely free of second thoughts regarding practicality. The design had what he wanted,[27] even if he had no valid reason to want it, and no one in the Admiralty showed the inclination to stop him.

---

[24] The *Hawkins* hull form evolved from work just carried out for *Courageous*. *Hawkins* had belt protection consisting of a 3-inch HT lamination but with more extensive coverage than in smaller cruisers, plus additional protective plating within the citadel. Like *Furious*, one of *Hawkins*'s sisters got sidetracked to completion as an aircraft carrier.

[25] Roberts, *Battlecruisers*, p 51.

[26] Early drafts show the design mounting only two turrets.

[27] He wrote to the design chief that "the more I consider the qualities of your design of the Big Light Battle Cruisers, the more I am impressed by its exceeding excellence and simplicity—*all the three vital requisites of gunpower, speed and draught of water* so well balanced!" See Roberts, *Battlecruisers*, p 51. How the hull's draft came to match Fisher's regard for speed and firepower (if in fact the message expresses an opinion he actually held) cannot be known.

For Fisher, the ships of the *Courageous* class were their own justification, sparing him an unpleasant question: Is 19,000 tons of useless ship so far superior to 0 tons of useful ship as to justify the expenditure?

Ultimately, all three ships found their route into usefulness as dedicated aviation platforms. Conversion gave them a form well suited to a coherent function, as well as a straightforward new rating—"aircraft carrier." They helped assure Britain's early lead in fast carrier capability, and they remained the Royal Navy's premier flattops until *Ark Royal* commissioned in 1938. Thus the misbegotten threesome proved that all's well that ends well—in design terms, anyway.

Figure 13. John Arbuthnot Fisher: what was going on inside that head?

WITHOUT ARMOR NONSENSE: ADMINISTRATION AS THE FATHER OF FLAWS

Frequently foisted into the battlecruiser category, the *Courageous* class with its shameless disregard for protection unfairly degrades the battlecruiser's already dubious reputation. While no other navies went to the same extremes as the British, some of them planned ships unmistakably destitute of armor.[28]

The United States

Lexington

- ❖ 41,000 tons
- ❖ 7-inch belt inclined at 11.5° and 1.5-inch upper belt
- ❖ 2.25-inch and 2-inch decks
- ❖ 9-inch barbette
- ❖ 11-inch turret face and 5-inch roof

By 1920, the Americans had largely forgotten how to make a cruiser, having gone without commissioning one since *Chester* in 1908 (3,750 tons, two 5-inch guns, 2-inch armor, 24 knots). The fleet's urgent need for large scouts gave rise to two new types, the dismal *Omaha*-class light cruiser and the *Lexington*-class battlecruiser—arguably more dismal than *Omaha*, and among the worst American designs of the century.

The gruesome path to approval—at one point, the design housed half its boilers above the armor belt, which is probably a bad thing for a ship relying on speed—didn't purge all virtues from the project. In fact, *Lexington* had much to commend. The turbo-electric propulsion allowed for an exceptional degree of subdivision while also providing excellent speed and useful range. The main battery of 16-inch/50-caliber rifles spoke for itself. However, one feature ruined everything.

Lexington's protection scheme crawled out of a Dali nightmare. Not merely thin, the armor sat scattered about the hull in disquieting contrast to the elegant arrangement gracing previous classes of American dreadnoughts; their all-or-nothing layout fixed a concentrated armor deck atop the belt armor with a splinter deck beneath. While *Lexington* retained the splinter layer, the thickest deck plating moved up to the weather deck where it covered only the inboard portion.[29] With this yawning gap be-

---

[28] Some would argue that the British had another clearly deficient design, *Renown*, but she was designed to match the armor of a previous battlecruiser (*Indefatigable*) which had not yet demonstrated any great vulnerability vis-à-vis the relatively small German guns.

[29] The specifications listed on *Lexington*'s "Spring Style" lack the standard entries for "protective" deck and "splinter" deck. Someone removed those words and replaced them with "upper" deck and "3rd" deck, which ably described the plating's location, but not its purpose.

tween deck and belt, a shell striking just above the side armor could plunge directly into the vitals with nothing thicker than splinter protection in its path.

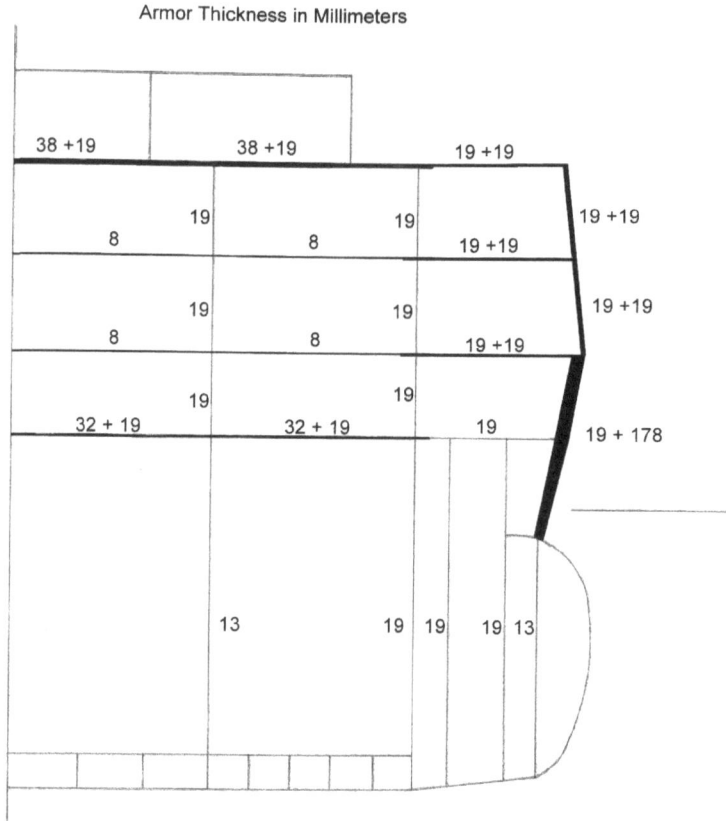

Figure 14. *Lexington* (Robert Lundgren)

The navy wanted these ships primarily for scouting. The campaign to secure battlecruiser allocations kicked off with a war game illustrating that powerful scouts could brush aside an enemy's weaker scouts—rather obvious, yet the publicity stunt succeeded. For confrontation with weaker scouts only (i.e., light cruisers), *Lexington* carried armor thicknesses best described as lavish. But the Americans understood quite well that battlecruisers would confront battlecruisers; Japan had four *Kongos* in service and rumor-fuls of new construction. *Kongo's* 14-inch guns posed a threat, and while *Lexington* might have prevailed in a one-on-one duel, her difference in size and vintage should rightly have assured a decisive advantage. As for the upcoming Japanese designs, they lagged behind *Lexington* in all-out speed, but shamed her in protection and surpassed her in firepower. The Americans knew *Lexington* would face 16-inch guns before her construction began. The mystery remains: how did such deficiencies become acceptable?

In 1901, work started on the massive *Pennsylvania*-class cruisers, carrying 8-inch guns and 6-inch belt armor. Two years later came the *Tennessee* class with 10-inch guns, but to meet the necessary speed and other requirements, designers shaved the belt to 5 inches. Large cruiser construction then ceased until *Lexington* came on the scene. Her 1919 drafts showed her with 16-inch guns and a 5-inch belt.[30] So while cruiser guns had gone from 8-inch to 16-inch, belt protection decreased. In contrast, American battleships during the same period went from 12-inch to 16-inch guns with belt armor increasing from 11-inch to 13.5-inch. Unlike the cruisers, battleships had enjoyed uninterrupted development.

Given this context, the battlecruiser's eventual 7-inch belt represents *a momentous upgrade*. It occurred after consultation with RN designer Stanley Goodall who came to the U.S. with documentation on the *Hood* design (12-inch belt) and Jutland damage reports indicating that German 11-inch and 12-inch guns had not penetrated armor thicker than 9-inch. If that explains *Lexington*'s 9-inch barbettes and 7-inch belt (inclined to perform like a 9-inch plate), it doesn't explain why anyone saw 12-inch guns as a suitable benchmark rather than 16-inch or at least 14-inch. In fact, if *Lexington* herself had mounted 14-inch guns, as planned in earlier versions of the design, significant weight would have become available for increased protection. It appears that *Lexington*'s designers found themselves bound within requirements for firepower, speed, and hull strength, then used whatever tonnage allowance remained to provide some armor—optimism at its worst.

The Soviet Union

Kronshtadt:

- ❖ 35,240 tons
- ❖ 9.2-inch belt inclined at 5°
- ❖ 3.6-inch and 1.2-inch decks
- ❖ 13.3-inch barbette
- ❖ 12.2-inch turret face and 5-inch roof

No dreadnought design gestated in a more inhospitable environment than Soviet Project 69, the *Kronshtadt*-class battlecruisers.

Domestic industry, still a cripple after the disasters of war and revolution, went through the 1920s without completing any new warships larger than 500 tons.[31] Not until 1935 did light cruiser construction resume, setting off a series of adventures in

---

[30] The *Tennessee* and *Pennsylvania* designs backed their belt protection with a sloped deck and coal stores, which *Lexington* lacked, but this was not a statistic easily revived in a planner's memory. One wonders how *Lexington*'s early drafts would have differed if *Tennessee* had repeated *Pennsylvania*'s 6-inch belt.

[31] Some pre-existing *Svetlana*-class cruiser hulls did sprint to completion in 1927, 1928, and 1932— that is, 13-18 years after keel-laying.

hull distortion (builders ignored the welding plan) and guns that "do not shoot." The navy couldn't build even a destroyer without major drama.

Politics, having removed all battleship enthusiasts from the fleet by 1930, focused naval planning on small units operating as adjuncts to the army. Stalin abruptly reversed his policy in 1935, and leaders who had risen to prominence on their denunciation of capital ships suddenly had to formulate a battleship policy. Design bureaus with decades of non-experience had to master the minutiae of large armored ships. Then in 1937, the Great Purge struck the navy, eliminating key personnel in industry, planning, and ship design.

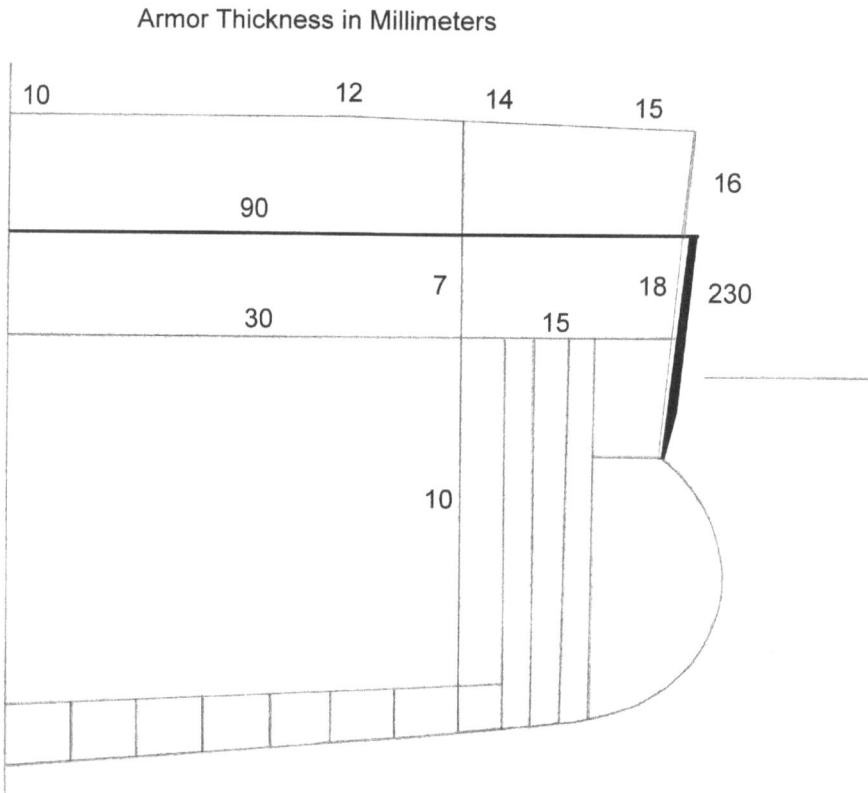

Figure 15. *Kronshtadt* (Robert Lundgren)

These events spun Soviet warship development into a chaotic whirl. Subjected to dead ends, false starts, restarts, and death by a thousand tweaks, dreadnought design eventually resolved into two finalized classes, the Project 23 battleships and the Project 69 battlecruisers. For *Kronshtadt*, finalization proved temporary because, though official policy had solidified behind dreadnought construction—Stalin loved battlecruisers—industrial challenges continued. Production difficulties slowed delivery of the 12-inch main battery; German-made 11-inch and 15-inch guns became an option. The armor scheme went basically unchanged, but the quality of protection remained a question mark. Soviet armor manufacture continued in a sorry state, and face-hardened armor (belt, turret face, etc.) suffered especially. The degree to which it would underperform is unknown.

Planners faced a lengthy list of opponents dictated by the Soviets' multiple naval sectors. In the Pacific, *Kongo*s lurked to spoil commerce-raiding efforts. *Kronshtadt* did show some superiority over *Kongo*, but hardly commensurate with the age and size difference. Project 69 neared the size of a treaty battleship like *Richelieu* but had nothing like *Richelieu*'s armor or weaponry.[32]

Operations in the North implied a German opponent. *Scharnhorst*, arguably the most flawed battleship of her generation, nevertheless carried much heavier protection than Project 69, and her modern 11-inch guns had good prospects against Soviet steel. A switch to 15-inch guns—planned for both *Kronshtadt* and *Scharnhorst*—increased Soviet hopes for penetrating heavy armor but ultimately represented a greater upgrade for *Scharnhorst*. Of course, *Bismarck* also carried 15-inch guns, and *Kronshtadt*'s instructions for such an encounter involved only retreat—perhaps the most sensible decision in the entire project.

Kronshtadt could vie for command of the Black Sea against *Yavuz*, Turkey's ex-German battlecruiser completed in 1912. The Turks had stockpiles of ammunition manufactured during World War I, but they may also have purchased new shells from Bofors in Sweden, and they had the capacity to manufacture their own modern types. Shell vintage may have made the difference against the Project 69 armor scheme. The prospects of an Italian push through the Straits raised concerns about Italy's veteran dreadnoughts, whose modernized 12.6-inch guns left no doubt about the ability to penetrate both belt and deck armor. Again, *Kronshtadt* ought to have enjoyed a comprehensive advantage against a competitor twenty-five years older and 8000 tons lighter.[33] Nevertheless, the Black Sea represented the one setting where the Soviets had realistic expectations for naval supremacy, and a design tailored to that scenario might have proved decisive in a naval war with Turkey.

Germany

Battlecruiser "O": 32,300 tons

- ❖ 7.2-inch belt and 3.2-inch upper belt
- ❖ 1.2-inch and 2.4-inch decks
- ❖ 7.2-inch barbette
- ❖ 8.4-inch turret face and 2-inch roof

---

[32] The 37,000-ton *Richelieu* (13.1-inch belt at 15.4°) had a broadside of 15,591 lbs to the 35,000-ton *Kronshtadt*'s 9326 lbs. Speed was about 32 knots in both ships.

[33] The Soviets never considered an encounter with *Littorio*, which spared them some unpleasant discussion.

The *Deutschland*-class pocket battleships seemed a promising model, and construction began on an enlarged follow-up. Work came to an abrupt stop when the French began their *Dunkerque* design, capable of crushing a pocket battleship, and the project restarted in a much more powerful form, the *Scharnhorst*-class battleships. The Germans made one more try at a pocket battleship, only to veer into another detour. The ensuing "OPQ" design, whose greatest achievement lay in inspiring the title of this essay, approximated *Scharnhorst* in size but diverged in major ways.

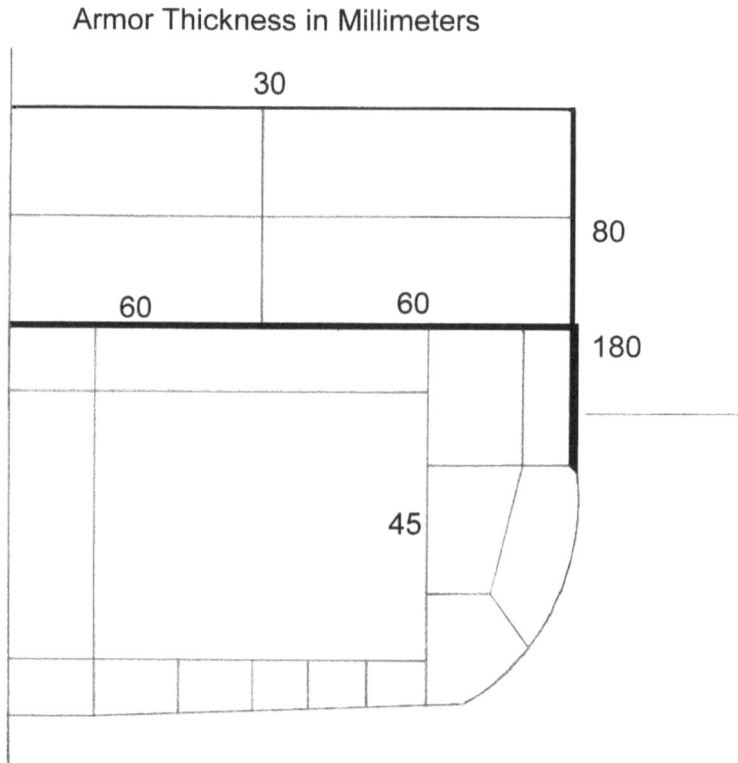

Figure 16. "O" (Robert Lundgren)

Unlike the earlier ship, Battlecruiser "O" had no aspirations to battleship-level protection. Planners intended that she engage nothing more intimidating than a heavy cruiser, outmaneuvering all larger opponents. The smallest opponents, aircraft, do not seem to have figured in the armor plan—even if an 8-inch shell had trouble against a 2-inch turret roof,[34] a dive-bomber would not find it so challenging. American 11,000-ton light cruisers carried 3-inch turret roofs.

Not only the armor scheme, but the fundamental concept had its foundation in wishful thought. Planners generated a vague idea of something that "O" might ac-

---

[34] German 15-inch turrets had various angled plates. In *Bismarck*, supposedly armored to battleship standards, the angles left her the turrets vulnerable to battleship guns at all ranges. An analogous vulnerability to cruiser guns may apply to "O," but existing sources do not record all the plate thicknesses.

complish but never integrated her mission with a realistic war scenario or a practical operational plan. The most important factor in the decision to build them may have been the anticipated availability of 15-inch guns originally meant for the *Scharnhorst*s, and not any tactical necessity. However, having ordered the ships, the fleet had to imagine a mission for them.

"O" was clearly a raider, and her mid-ocean depredations would coincide with sorties by carrier-battleship task forces that would crush enemy convoys and devour enemy warships piecemeal as they darted about the ocean in frenzied dismay.[35] The logistical details for Germany's diesel-powered battleships operating with turbine-powered carriers (and for the "O's" simultaneous sortie) avoided any serious study, as did the procedure for this collection of vessels to break out into the sea-lanes and then break back into their home ports—all this in a world of increasingly capable electronics, increasingly powerful aircraft, and increasingly numerous British men-of-war.

Fantasy mumbled that such problems would be overcome. Reality would have responded to "O" with aerial attacks and convoy escorts more powerful than an aging heavy cruiser. The Americans, for example, had already started their *Alaska*-class cruiser project. *Alaska* had speed roughly equal to "O's" and a nasty battery of 12-inch guns. Had the "O" class actually progressed to completion, the British would have developed their own specific counters, and since studies had shown that large cruisers armed with 9.2-inch guns cost as much as a battleship, the counter would likely have mounted large-caliber guns of its own. Yet the proliferation of carrier aviation may have obviated such projects, reducing "O" to a solitary object of target practice for British airmen.

Historically, the German Navy couldn't identify the mission for the largest ships it completed, the *Bismarck*s and *Scharnhorst*s, and their wartime operations became extemporized gambles that ceased to offer prospects of success after mid-1941. A similar lack of mission for the Never-Were units hardly surprises. Had "O," "P," and "Q" somehow reached completion, they would have given the fleet a set of long-ranged, heavily armed ships suited to no imaginable purpose.

Conclusion

Lexington, *Kronshtadt*, and "O" enjoyed individual paths to inadequacy. The natural temptation to crown one as disaster-in-chief must end in acknowledgment that each was uniquely suited to its own brand of failure. Yet as a group, they shared the good fortune that turned them aside from completion and spared each from becoming synonymous with "death trap." The Germans canceled "O" before construction began; the onset of Operation Barbarossa ended *Kronshtadt* prior to launching; *Lexington* and one of her sister ships avoided a treaty-induced death sentence only by converting to aircraft carriers.

---

[35] The enemy would be Britain and her allies. The *Kriegsmarine* had graduated from merely countering the French.

While retrospect might try to fault the designers, men who simply executed the requirements handed to them, first blame rests on a broader base: organizational failure. As these ships—and *Renown* and *Courageous*, for that matter—starkly illustrate, administrative deficiencies create an incubator for bad designs. Even a healthy, growing fleet like the United States Navy after World War I could generate a blind spot big enough to house a 40,000-ton embarrassment, while Admiral Fisher proved that one unchecked individual could wreak momentous mischief, even in the world's premier navy. For the Germans, the problem arose from an institution-wide delusion that justified growth for growth's sake with no realistic application.

The Soviets compounded these hazards into one all-encompassing blight, as Stalin proved by dragging his navy back into Without-Armor-Nonsense a second time. It was his authority alone that pushed Project 82 (the *Stalingrad* class 12-inch "heavy cruisers") into construction after World War II—the world's final dreadnought construction program. Project 82 actually began before the 1941 German invasion as the Soviets decided to build an 8-inch cruiser somewhat larger than *Tallinn* (ex-*Lützow*, newly purchased from the Germans). The typical, tortured process of Soviet development inflated the ship till it reached 35,500 tons and resembled *Kronshtadt* in a number of features. Though the armor scheme differed, the level of protection remained similar. The belt thinned to 7.2 inches but angled at 15°; the armor deck thinned to 2.8 inches but enjoyed the cover of 2-inch upper hull plating.

In Stalin's mind, this design represented an intimidating coast-defense unit. As enemy carrier battle fleets approached the Soviet coast, *Stalingrad* would lurk nearby and pounce on any lesser cruiser that strayed from the company of its fleet-mates—or something like that. No operational plan dictated how *Stalingrad* would get into gun range of any target without first coming into range of enemy aircraft. Theoretically, the ship would have cover from Soviet land-based fighters, despite the difficulties of coordinating such operations and the very limited range of the planes. Aircraft aside, the ship would risk encounters with opponents more challenging than a wayward light cruiser—*Alaska* with her 12-inch guns, *Vanguard* with her 15-inchers, or American battleships with 16-inchers. There was no realistic scenario in which Project 82 could prosper.

But Stalin prized battlecruisers above reality. Fittingly, the project died with him. In this way, the day of the frail battlecruiser came to an end, years after the age of battleships had passed.

Figure 17. The British kept their "fully armoured battlecruiser" *Vanguard* in
   commission postwar to counter Soviet cruisers.

Who Killed the Battlecruiser?

In October 1917, the Germans commissioned *Hindenburg*, and an era came to a close. *Hindenburg* was the last pure battlecruiser ever completed.

For a type that generated such excitement and demanded such vast expenditures, the battlecruiser suffered a surprisingly abrupt demise. What was it that brought the romance to an end?

On 31 May 1916, the main British and German fleets clashed for the first and only time in World War I. The Battle of Jutland confirmed British supremacy at sea, but at a terrible cost. The Royal Navy's losses included three battlecruisers (*Queen Mary*, *Indefatigable*, and *Invincible*) with 3,314 of their crewmen—only 28 survived—when subjected to heavy gunfire from German battlecruisers at ranges up to 16,000 yards. The Germans also lost a battlecruiser (*Lützow*, with 116 men), but only after a numerous shell hits, torpedo damage, and the crew's protracted struggle against progressive flooding—a testimony, in fact, to extreme ruggedness. Nevertheless, the shock of Britain's loss eclipsed all else, and by the time the victors wrote the history of World War I, the battlecruiser's reputation bore a permanent stain.

Yet there remained an event far more devastating for the battlecruiser, as the pen proved mightier than the sword. The Washington Treaty of 1922, one of the more successful arms treaties in history, doomed more capital ships than any battle did. America alone scrapped or converted six partly complete battlecruisers. Britain canceled orders for four ships that were battlecruisers in name (if not in design). Japan abandoned its own extensive programs, four ships under construction and four more planned. The treaty, which also included France and Italy, created an international "holiday" that put off new construction for ten years.

The treaty system broke down amid the imperialism of the 1930s. Nevertheless, only the Germans and Soviets (non-signatories of the Washington Treaty) pursued serious programs for lightly armored capital ships. Both fleets intended their battlecruisers for commerce warfare, and—it must be said—both fleets lacked anything like a coherent strategy to make that mission practical. For a navy trying to play catch-up in the naval race, the battlecruiser tantalized with its potential to vex the premier maritime powers—a specious promise that confused tactical speed with strategic mobility and ignored such novelties as radio and the aeroplane. Perhaps it was for the best that none of these units reached completion.

The treaty signatories, having enjoyed the luxury of decades with established naval strength and perspective, were not so easily misled. With the limited numbers of capital ships that could be built, specialization gave place to flexibility—designs that could operate with other fast units like aircraft carriers or commerce cruisers but could also go toe-to-toe in a battle-line brawl. Navies in the know understood that the pure battlecruiser was dead.

Figure 18. America's battlecruisers died in the best possible place—on paper. *Lexington* had the good fortune, after the demise of her original design, to be launched and completed as an aircraft carrier.

THE FIRST SHALL BE LAST: *KONGO* IN THE JAPANESE DESIGN PROCESS[36]

The armored cruiser stood as a metaphor for the Imperial Japanese Navy itself—able to confront a nominally superior foe and, by virtue of speed and crew skill, to win. Despite this affinity, the road to the *Kongos*—Japan's first and final true battle-cruisers—had more than its share of blind curves and potholes.

Authorization for the first domestically built armored cruisers came shortly before the Russian war, but actual construction straggled behind. Work began on the *Tsu-kuba* and *Kurama* classes by 1907, but it eventually fell to the 1910 and 1911 programs to rescue the four *Kongos* which had spent as long as seven years in administrative limbo. Delays resulted from the usual issues of industrial limitation, wartime urgency, and postwar purse strings, complicated by the fact that technological frontiers had advanced even faster for cruisers than they had for battleships.

Table 2. Japanese Armored Cruiser Authorization, 1903-1907

Program	Authorized as	Eventual name and date of naming
Third Fleet Extension Program, 1903	No. 1 Armored Cruiser	*Ibuki* (1905)
	No. 2 Armored Cruiser	*Haruna* (1913)
	No. 3 Armored Cruiser	*Kirishima* (1911)
1904 Wartime Warship Construction Program	SHI GO Armored Cruiser	*Tsukuba* (1905)
	CHU GO Armored Cruiser	*Ikoma* (1905)
	IN GO Armored Cruiser	*Kurama* (1905)
	BO GO Armored Cruiser	*Hiei* (1911)
1907 Post Russo-Japanese War Equipment Program	I GO Armored Cruiser	*Kongo* (1911)

The Dreadnought Revolution capped a century of rampant innovation. Steam propulsion, armor, quick-firing guns, and finally rangefinders and other fire-control mechanization—the world's fleets labored to blend modern ingredients into a practical recipe for naval success, sometimes with glaring failure. The British mounted sails on a low-freeboard hull and watched as HMS *Captain* capsized. Italian deliberations on the nature of shipboard protection led to building the *Italia*-class battleships without belt armor. America's cruiser *Vesuvius* carried 15-inch pneumatic guns that could not elevate or train. Most of the wrong turns met their logical dead ends by the 1890s; battleship ideas crystallized into a conventional form, and the armored cruiser emerged as a promising vehicle for a variety of roles, including participation in the line of battle.

---

[36] Excerpted from a larger work-in-progress, *Cresting Wave: Japanese Battleships of World War II.*

Like the other major fleets, the Imperial Japanese Navy knew the factors militating for battleship-caliber weaponry in all capital ships. Accordingly, *Tsukuba* and *Ikoma* of 1905, the first products of domestic armored cruiser construction, mounted a 12-inch main battery. Even before their launch, work began on an improved design; *Kurama* escalated from a 6-inch secondary battery to turreted 8-inchers, while her sister *Ibuki* added turbine propulsion that promised to give future ships a more competitive speed. Planners certainly saw the combination of 12-inch and 8-inch guns as an advance in firepower, putting the ship on a par with the most powerful battleships, but it also revealed an inconsistency. Since the large-caliber gun had emerged as the premier weapon, the logical step would have been a uniform 12-inch armament. Specifications for the next project continued to hedge on the firepower issue.

- ❖ Displacement: 18,650 tons

- ❖ Dimensions: 541 x 80 x 26.5 feet

- ❖ Propulsion: 44,000 shp = 25 knots

- ❖ Armament: four 12-inch/45 guns, eight 10-inch guns, ten 4.7-inch guns, five torpedo tubes

- ❖ Armor: 7-inch belt, 2-inch deck

Figure 19. *Tsukuba's* good looks didn't make her a match for the true battlecruisers.

The boost to 25 knots represented a significant improvement, but the 10-inch battery represented not as much a gain in firepower as Japan's hesitation on the brink of the all-big-gun revolution.

In 1906, Britain began building the 17,373-ton *Invincible* with its 25-knot speed and the firepower of eight 12-inch guns, and Japan saw its newest capital ships shunted into obsolescence. The British trumpeted this upheaval of cruiser standards by officially re-rating *Invincible* as a "battle cruiser," terminology soon adopted by the Japanese, though it rather flattered *Tsukuba* and *Kurama*.[37] More substantively, initiatives got underway to return Japan to the forefront of warship design. *Invincible* and her two sister ships inspired pleas in the Diet for a Japanese trio,[38] but this was the same year in which the navy failed to negotiate a budget for any new capital ships. Even in 1907, the year when the Imperial Japanese National Defense Policy established the United States as the navy's "budgetary enemy" and the Naval Strength Requirement set the stage for the famous 8-8 Fleet effort, no funds for new construction became available. A new, catchy title for the project—Cruiser "I-Go"—wasn't enough to win support.

While politicos made their best play for money, designers busied themselves with a new batch of drawings, thirty studies that bridged the gap between *Kurama* (Design B-15) and the eventual *Kongo* (Design B-46). Most effort went into *Invincible*-ish ideas, ships under 19,000 tons with a speed near 26 knots and a battery of eight 12-inch guns, including two mounts arranged *en échelon*. This arrangement carried over into some ten-gun versions, but ultimately the centerline armament seen in USS *Michigan* gained favor. A boost in firepower came in the form of 50-caliber guns rather than the 45-caliber of *Tsukuba* and *Invincible*. Plans moved toward a finalized design.

Then Britain again ruined it all, laying down in 1909 the battlecruiser *Lion*— at 26,270 tons with 13.5-inch guns, a monumental leap in size and capability. Japanese frustration gelled into a resolve both ambitious and pragmatic. Japanese design would no longer lag behind foreign developments, and if Japanese industry lacked the foundation for super-dreadnought aspiration, there was help available from a good source—Japan's friend and the source of Japan's frustration, Britain.

Almost the entire battle line for the Russian war had come from British shipyards, and Armstrong alone had supplied six capital ships. Vickers, though, had earned respect with *Mikasa* and *Katori*, and the company had won a contract to build one of the *Lion*-class ships for the Royal Navy. Both firms had investments in Japanese industry, and both tendered proposals for the new ship.

Vickers came out on top. As a key point in the agreement, the design and construction process would involve a substantial contingent of Japanese specialists: designers and workmen, both naval and civilian, eventually two hundred men in total. The project in fact represented a three-fold venture, of which building the ship was merely one part. The Japanese intended it additionally as a classroom for its personnel and as a benchmark for the industrial advances Japan had yet to achieve before claiming equality with the Western powers. Consequently, Vickers would build one unit and provide necessary plans and materials to allow Japanese yards to construct sister

---

[37] The Japanese officially adopted the term on 28 August 1912, making *Kongo* a "battlecruiser" three months after her launching.

[38] The navy actually wanted four units, in keeping with its tactical formations, but the threesome perhaps represented a foot in the door.

ships. Working closely with the Japanese personnel, Thomas George Owens[39] over-saw a series of studies which Vickers presented on 30 July 1910. This formed the basis for the *Kongo* design.

Table 3. Key dates for Japan's battlecruiser program.

Date	Event
January–March 1905	Keels laid for *Tsukuba* and *Ikoma* (13,750 tons; four 12-inch, twelve 6-inch guns)
1905–07	Keels laid for *Kurama* and *Ibuki* (14,636 tons; four 12-inch, eight 8-inch guns)
February–Apr 1906	Keels laid for *Invincible* class, first all-big-gun armored cruisers (17,373 tons; eight 12-inch guns)
19 November 1909	British 13.5-inch gun first proved
29 November 1909	Keel laid for *Lion* (26,270 tons; eight 13.5-inch guns)
January 1910	US fires 14-inch prototype gun
17 January 1911	Keel laid for *Kongo*
April–September 1911	Keels laid for *Texas* and *New York* (27,000 tons; ten 14-inch guns)
20 June 1912	Keel laid for *Tiger* (28,430 tons; eight 13.5-inch guns)

Vickers offered several options, such as adding a knot of speed, widening the main belt, and increasing the main battery to ten guns via two triple turrets. However, the most important options concerned the main battery caliber. Each design came with weight breakdowns for three variations: one armed with 12-inch guns, one armed with 14-inch guns, and one with 12-inch guns mounted in 14-inch turrets to allow future upgrade.[40]

This introduces one of the thorny issues of the *Kongo* project. Since it was *Lion*'s super-dreadnought weaponry that started the Japanese on this new project, the consideration of a 12-inch battery—albeit 50-caliber—implies significant reservations among the decision-makers, who knew also that the Americans had begun a 14-inch design, while rumors proliferated about something similar brewing in Germany.

Other weighty factors were in play. Japan remained intensely aware of its industrial limits, even as it struggled to expand those limits. The difference between a 12-inch gun and a 14-inch gun seems minor when described in bore diameter, but the industrial challenge shows more proportionally in the weights for the guns (69 tons versus 85 tons) and their shells (882 lbs versus 1,400 lbs).

---

[39] The Vickers chief designer, who upon knighthood took the name Sir George Thurston. The Thurston notebooks provide numerous studies for Japanese warships, but no drawings for proposed dreadnoughts.

[40] Armament weights: 12-inch guns, 3,600 tons; 12-inch guns in 14-inch turrets, 3,695 tons; 14-inch guns, 4,045 tons.

Table 4. Vickers Proposals

Design	No. 472	No. 473	No. 474	No. 475
Length pp[41]	646'-0"	656'-0"	620'-0"	605'-0"
Breadth ext[42]	92'-0"	92'-0"	90'-0"	90'-0"
Molded depth	43'-6"	43'-6"	43'-6"	43'-6"
Draft mean	27'-6"	27'-6"	27'-6"	27'-6"
Displacement	26,250 tons	26,500 tons	25,600 tons	24,900 tons
Machinery	59,000 shp = 27 knots	58,000 shp = 27 knots	60,000 shp = 27 knots	60,500 shp = 27 knots
Fuel	Coal 1,100 tons normal, 4,000 tons full; oil 1,000 tons	Coal 1,100 tons normal; oil 1,000 tons	Coal 1,100 tons normal, 4,000 tons full; oil 1,000 tons	Coal 1,100 tons normal, 4,000 tons full; oil 1,000 tons
Armament (for all versions)	❖ Eight 12-inch B.L. guns; 80 rounds ❖ Sixteen 6-inch Q.F. guns; 120 rounds ❖ Eight 3-inch/40 guns; 300 rounds ❖ Eight 3-inch short guns; 300 rounds ❖ Four 6.5-mm machine guns; 15,000 rounds ❖ Eight 21-inch submerged torpedo tubes, two torpedoes per tube			
Armor and protection (for all versions)	❖ Main belt 8-inch, fore and aft 3-inch ❖ Underbelt 3-inch ❖ Upper belt 6-inch ❖ Casemate belt 6-inch ❖ Casemate roof 2 x 0.625-inch ❖ Flying deck 2 x 0.5-inch ❖ Main deck maximum 1-inch ❖ Middle deck in citadel 0.75-inch, aft 2 x 1-inch ❖ Lower deck forward 2 x 0.75-inch ❖ Barbettes 9-inch ❖ Conning tower 10-inch ❖ Observer tower 6-inch			

Gunnery experts could advocate the 12-inch gun based on its 50-caliber length and consequently higher muzzle velocity. Compared to slower 14-inch shells, the 12-inch shell trajectories would not arch as high and so would stay longer on level with the target to create a higher percentage of hits. Since a smaller gun might also fire more quickly, the 12-incher deserved consideration.

---

[41] Length can be measured in three ways: overall (oa), waterline (wl), and between perpendiculars (pp—in simple terms, the distance between the bow at the waterline and the rudder shaft).

[42] Extreme breadth is the width of the hull at its widest point, including the thickness of the plates themselves.

Toward the end of 1909, Japan's naval attaché in Britain, Commander Hiroharu Kato (perhaps better known as Kanji Kato, a leader of the "Fleet Faction" that welcomed war against the United States in the 1930s), learned about RN trials comparing 12-inch/50 and 13.5-inch/45 guns. Given a copy of the official report, he became an advocate for increased caliber. Barrel erosion in the 12-inch gun would limit its life to one third what the 13.5-incher achieved, and accuracy was inferior as well—an especially damning factor, as it was the 12-inch gun's prospects for a greater number of hits that argued most forcefully in its favor.

However, the 13.5-inch gun had its drawbacks, including the impending arrival of 14-inch guns in America—the Japanese did not want to be one-upped again. Kato traveled to the Coventry Ordnance Works, where Reginald Bacon, a retired admiral who had served as *Dreadnought*'s first commander, persuasively argued for a 14-inch gun. (In fact, he had a 14-inch/42 design of his own to recommend.) Other RN gunnery experts expressed similar views, which helped solidify Kato's arguments. In the end, even the most conservative Imperial Japanese Navy (IJN) leaders accepted that Bigger was Better—a maxim that would dominate the IJN to its last days.[43] The date of the official decision, though, remains unknown. Existing clues are not easily reconciled.

The navy's gunnery staff received the official report of the British comparative gun trials in August 1910. Vickers, instructed to refine Design No. 472, presented No. 472C in October 1910. The specifications for this High Speed Armoured Cruiser "I" included the following notation for armament: "8 - 43 Type (14") 45 cal." It also listed the armament weight at 4,175 tons, which matches closest to the 472 variant with 14-inch guns. This design became the basis for the final contract specifications.

Unfortunately, this doesn't resolve the gun mystery. The final set of figures in Thurston's notebook removes any mention of the 14-inch caliber.

Cruiser "I" Japanese *Kongo*

- ❖ Dimensions: 653'-6" pp, 695'-6" wl, 704'-0" oa x 92'-0" x 27'-6" mean

- ❖ Molded Depth: 43'-3"

- ❖ Displacement: 27,500 tons

- ❖ Machinery: 64,000 shp, 27.5 knots

- ❖ Fuel: Coal 1,100 tons normal, 4,000 tons full; oil 1,000 tons

- ❖ Complement: 1,100

---

[43] The Japanese would become the first to build a battleship with 16-inch guns and the first (and only) to build a battleship with 18-inch guns. When striving for a way to improve on *Yamato*'s nine 18.1-inch guns, planners would settle on six 20.1-inch guns, which seems impressive though it actually reduced the broadside from 28,968 lbs to 25,794 lbs.

Armament:

- ❖ Eight 43 Type guns; 80 rounds

- ❖ Sixteen 6-inch/50 guns; 120 rounds.

- ❖ Eight 3-inch/40 guns; 300 rounds.

- ❖ Eight 3-inch short guns; 300 rounds.

- ❖ Four 6.5-mm machine guns; 15,000 rounds.

- ❖ Eight 21-inch submerged torpedo tubes; two torpedoes per tube

Armor and Protection:[44]

- ❖ Observer tower: 6-inch

- ❖ Conning tower: 10-inch

- ❖ Main belt: 8-inch, 3-inch fore and aft

- ❖ Upper belt: 6-inch

- ❖ Casemate belt: 6-inch

- ❖ Underbelt: 3-inch

- ❖ Barbettes: 9-inch

- ❖ Flying deck: 1.5-inch NS[45]

- ❖ Upper deck: maximum 0.75-inch MS[46]

- ❖ Main deck: maximum forward 1-inch NS

- ❖ Middle deck: 0.75-inch NS, forward 1.5-inch NS, aft 2-inch NS

- ❖ Magazine sides and ends: maximum 1-inch NS

- ❖ Battery rears: 0.75-inch NS

- ❖ Battery divisions: 1-inch NS

Weights (all in tons):

- ❖ Hull and fittings: 9,335

- ❖ Auxiliary machinery: 330

- ❖ Machinery: 4,460

---

[44] Armor figures are converted from pounds to inches (40 lbs. = 1 inch). NS = nickel steel. MS = mild steel.

[45] NS: supra.

[46] MS: supra.

- ❖ Coal: 1,100

- ❖ Armor: 4,664

- ❖ Protection: 2,271

- ❖ Armament: 3,918

- ❖ Electrical equipment: 245

- ❖ Equipment: 1,006

- ❖ Margin: 171

Still the 3,918-ton armament hints at a 14-inch battery, but later material (including the signed contract of 17 October 1910) indicate 43 Type 12-inch guns. Vickers laid *Kongo*'s keel in January 1911. The 14-inch prototype, completed the following month, began its testing in March. Some researchers claim the Navy Technical Department did not authorize the switch to 14-inch guns until 29 November 1911, but a Japanese document from that date offers one explanation for the apparent disagreement of sources. It says, "Henceforth the 14-inch guns are to be referred to as 12-inch Type 43."[47] If this practice had been surreptitiously underway since July, it might explain the removal of the 14-inch notation in Thurston's notebook and the subsequent 12-inch references.

In any case, this leaves two possibilities: either *Kongo* had been under construction for ten months before the design switched to 14-inch guns, or the Japanese authorized a 14-inch *Kongo* months before the first 14-inch gun ever fired. The latter does not seem outrageous; the British committed to *Lion* before the 13.5-inch gun proved itself, as the prototype completed trials in the same month the ship began construction. In the absence of certainty, the best guess says that Japan authorized a 14-inch battery between August and October 1910.

A second, and simpler, question revolves around *Kongo*'s relationship to other designs, given the practice of design cross-breeding among the private shipyards as well as the Royal Navy. Several sources find a relative in HMS *Erin*, built at Vickers as *Reshadieh* for the Ottoman fleet. However, Vickers built her to Armstrong design 698C, Josiah Perrett's work, so Thurston provided only secondary input at most.

Likewise, rumors routinely link *Kongo* with the Royal Navy's "Big Cats," *Lion* and *Tiger*, despite an absence of evidence. *Lion* inspired the *Kongo* project only in a most general sense, and Thurston had no personal involvement with *Lion*. In fact, few points of similarity present themselves—two ships mounting four centerline turrets on a battlecruiser hull.

But according to theory, *Kongo* has *Tiger* as her cousin, both being refined *Lion*s. Again, the theory subsists on the superficial commonalities, such as the 6-inch secondary battery. In reality, *Tiger*'s escalation from 4-inch to 6-inch guns came not from

---

[47] The world knew the actual caliber of *Kongo*'s guns prior to her launching in May 1912.

copying *Kongo* but in response to ongoing dissatisfaction among many RN officers regarding the smaller weapon. Complaints became prominent by 1909, pointing out that the 6-inch gun could endanger enemy destroyers at a longer range, but more importantly, it offered more chance to inflict appreciable harm on battleship targets. Thus 6-inch became the new standard starting with the 1911 battleship program (the *Iron Duke* class, whose growth in tonnage resulted largely from this secondary battery) and the corresponding battleship project—*Tiger*. *Kongo* had nothing to do with it.

Similarly, the disposition of the main battery in *Kongo* looks to be an improvement on *Lion's*, with *Tiger* then following the Japanese example. However, early drafts of the *Tiger* design show her guns mounted fore and aft in tight, superfiring pairs; then designers found that a wider spacing allowed for increased arcs of fire and easier accommodation of her torpedo battery. Again, the British were finding their own solutions to design issues.

Figure 20. Vickers has installed the wooden backing for *Kongo's* belt armor. (Boris Lemachko Collection)

Kongo and *Tiger* represent simultaneous efforts by designers who often shared notes, but no deeper relationship exists. Documentation on *Tiger* does acknowledge Japanese influence, but it involved only a single feature—the 3-inch underbelt[48]—and

---

[48] The comment on the 3-inch strake in the *Tiger* Ship's Cover —"This plan is adopted in modern Japanese vessels and is a result of experience in the late war"—is the document's only Japanese reference.

the two designs show more contrasts than commonalities: differing armor schemes, differing underwater protection, differing torpedo armaments, etc.

Kongo, the first dreadnought to mount 14-inch guns, commissioned in Britain on 13 August 1916. Three sister ship orders went to Japanese yards—*Hiei* at Yokosuka Naval Yard, then *Kirishima* and *Haruna* at the two premier private yards, Mitsubishi Nagasaki and Kawasaki Kobe respectively—each unit progressively less dependent on British materials. Japan's next capital ship design, the massive *Fuso*, was domestically designed and built. The *Kongo* project had served its multi-purpose.

Yet *Kongo*'s role in Japanese warship design didn't end there. World events assured she would remain a frontline unit, and she became the oldest dreadnought to serve as an active combatant in World War II. This forced the Japanese to provide elaborate upkeep. The Washington Treaty imposed a numerical inferiority on Japan's capital ships vis-à-vis the rival Americans, but it also permitted improvements for existing units. So, starting in the late 1920s, *Kongo* and her sisters underwent rebuilds that augmented their armor. Officially re-rated as battleships, they couldn't match up against true battleships in a gunfight, but they could still take advantage of their speed against America's sluggish battle line, even though the armor upgrade cost them a knot or so. The underlying tactical thought differed little from that which succeeded in the Russo-Japanese War, but the obvious need to trump American superiority forced the Japanese to seek new solutions.

The result was a precisely choreographed evolution commonly known as the Decisive Battle plan, which featured a massed torpedo attack during the night before the battle-line engagement. The hope invested in this attack grew going into the 1930s as the *Takao*s gave the fleet another set of powerful heavy cruisers to spearhead the assault and new technologies bore fruit: the Long Lance torpedo, specialized night optics, improved starshells. However, the tempest of treaty negotiations failed to secure the 10:7 cruiser ratio Japan wanted, and the Americans recommitted themselves to heavy cruiser construction, ships that might provide an effective shield for the American battle line. By mid-decade, Japanese planners decided on an extraordinary measure—they cast the *Kongo*s in the role of cruiser-killers to push the nighttime torpedo attack to successful completion.

For the second time, the old ships went into the yards for renovation, the changes this time even more extensive.[49] New propulsion machinery and lengthened hulls boosted the ships to faster speeds than ever before. Improved weaponry, improved subdivision, eventually some more armor—yet even these measures seemed a stopgap, given the ships' advancing age. The fleet needed something new, a fast ship with sufficient communications and the power to dominate American heavy cruisers.

---

[49] *Hiei* went through a unique process. In accord with the London Treaty, she first underwent demotion to a training ship with the removal of some guns and armor. Reduction of her propulsion machinery dropped her to 18 knots, supposedly (rumors said otherwise, despite what the treaty demanded). In any case, all restrictions lapsed with the treaty, and by 1940 she regained a configuration not unlike that of her sisters.

Figure 21. An early view of *Haruna*. (Boris Lemachko Collection)

Figure 22. As a training ship during the interwar era, *Hiei* had her belt armor removed. (Boris Lemachko Collection)

By walking away from the 1936 London Conference, the Japanese gained the right to build such a ship and whatever else they wanted, and they celebrated their freedom by formulating the secret Circle-3 Program (to include *Yamato* and *Musashi*, the carriers *Shokaku* and *Zuikaku*, and more than sixty other units). The international rumor mill began grinding at once. *Jane's* closed out 1936 with mundane conjecture about four 35,000-ton ships, but with Japan's refusal of the 14-inch gun limit in March 1937, the *New York Times* acknowledged ongoing whispers about battleships wider than the Panama Canal. By year's end, *Il giornale d'Italia* boldly specified three Japanese ships of 46,000 tons each. A succession of Japanese denials failed to quiet the speculation, so in February 1938, France, Britain, and America petitioned Tokyo to divulge its naval construction plans and calm the worries about monster ships, not to mention British fears about commerce-raiding pocket battleships carrying 10-inch or 12-inch guns. Tokyo declined.

The naval race had begun. Almost lost amid the prevailing talk of gargantuan dreadnought designs was the rumor about pocket battleships. It flourished in the shadowy corners of naval intelligence until authorities like *Jane's* and the U.S. War Department pinpointed the names and characteristics for an entire class of ships that existed nowhere outside the imagination. Not waiting for further details, the U.S. Navy had launched official studies into its own super-cruiser design less than a month after Japan snubbed the Western information request, then quietly slipped the project into its vast "2-Ocean Navy Building Program" of July 1940. The Navy Department announced that the largest cruisers in the program would displace 15,000 to 20,000 tons like the *Baltimore*-class heavy cruisers, nothing likely to gain Tokyo's notice when the same program included seven 55,000-ton battleships.

Drafting began in 1939 on project V-16, Japan's "Super-A cruiser," a ship of 32,000 standard tons with nine 12.2-inch guns, sixteen 3.9-inch guns, and a speed of 33 knots—not the commerce raider feared by the West, but the cruiser-killer intended for Decisive Battle—to be fully drawn up by 1941. On 7 January 1941, the Naval General Staff reshuffled the details of its Circle-5 and Circle-6 proposals. Circle-5 would now include two V-16 units, order numbers 795 and 796 to be built to the Basic Design No. B-65 by Kure Naval Yard. Upon completion, the pair would form Division 8 of the Second Fleet (the scouting fleet, the key player in the planned night torpedo attack on the American battle line). Four more ships would follow in the Circle-6 Program and join the Second Fleet as Division 7, or so said the plans.

The Circle-6 Program hadn't reached its final form when, in September 1941, the high command agreed to put it on hold. With war looming, construction programs underwent a thorough revision, postponing the Circle-5 super-cruisers on 6 November 1941 to focus on more immediate needs. The Americans had a different approach to crisis; ten days after the Pearl Harbor attack, the U.S. Navy announced the keel-laying of the large cruiser *Alaska*, the first of six ships displacing 25,000 tons. This confirmed any suspicions the Japanese may have had that their enemy might build the same sort of ships they were building. Revelations about *Alaska's* actual characteristics caused a review of B-65, which no longer had superiority over its anticipated opponent. An armament increase to six 14-inch guns, along with a proportional upgrade in armor, pushed the design displacement up to 40,000 tons—a full-sized battleship. Prospects for V-16 withered, and then the Battle of Midway delivered the *coup de grâce*. Circle-6 officially died, and no super-cruisers figured in any subsequent programs.

That left the *Kongo* class without a successor, and the ships labored on. Within six months after Midway, two *Kongo*s fell victim to night battles, but hardly as the Decisive Battle forecast. *Hiei* suffered the indignity of crippling at the hands of the heavy cruisers she was intended to crush; yet she had more luck than *Kirishima*, who ran into a pair of modern battleships and a barrage of 16-inch shells.[50] After two more years of war and increasing desperation in the face of overwhelming American strength, *Kongo* succumbed to a submarine attack while trying to withdraw to the Japanese home islands. *Haruna* completed the journey only to be bombed while sitting in port idle and helpless.

And in the end, Japan's last armored cruisers became an apt symbol of the Imperial Navy's fortunes.

Figure 23. *Kirishima* in 1938. (History on CD-ROM)

---

[50] She suffered twenty hits, a hammering that caused her to abruptly capsize just as her crew was abandoning her. The traditional Western accounts about nine 16-inch hits and scuttling derive from a single uninformed source. See *Warship International*, Vol. 44, No. 4, 2007, pp 329-331.

THE MIGHTIEST MIGHT-HAVE-BEEN

Often lost in the naval histories, even in records of the battleship, is a design that might have become the most dominating dreadnought of World War I. Not *Queen Elizabeth* or *Royal Sovereign* or *Hood*. Not *Bayern* or *Sachsen* or even the *Ersatz Yorck*.

Perhaps on the coattails of Tsushima's humiliation, the Tsar's dreadnoughts elicit meager regard, and a project that never reached completion has little hope to venture out of the footnotes. The *Izmail*-class battlecruisers began construction, and if fate had shown enough charity to bring a ship to completion, *Izmail* might have stood as one of history's finest dreadnoughts.

- ❖ *Hindenburg*: 26,500 tons, 12-inch belt armor, eight 12-inch and fourteen 5.9-inch guns, 27 knots

- ❖ *Izmail*: 32,500 tons, 9.5-inch belt armor, twelve 14-inch and twenty-four 5.1-inch guns, 28 knots

Germany's *Hindenburg* often garners votes as the best battlecruiser of the Great War. *Izmail* was laid down the same year as *Hindenburg* (1913) and launched the same year (1915). The complexities of their armor schemes preclude a definitive comparison, but the general advantage lies with *Hindenburg* despite her lesser size. What *Izmail* has going for her is her ability to deal hammering blows to even the stoutest target.

Russian shells possessed the three key features distinguishing the premier armor-piercing shells of World War I. The metallurgy of their armor-piercing caps and shell bodies maximized results against enemy armor. In postwar trials, prewar Russian shells matched the latest British "Greenboys" (designed after the lessons of Jutland) in defeating armor while remaining whole enough to burst properly. The Russians used trinitrotuolene (TNT) as their explosive, rather than the picric acid used by several other navies. The impact of shell against armor usually triggered picric acid, causing the shell to burst before piercing deeply into the target. TNT behaved much more reliably—an important factor because the Russians also had a delay fuze well before some other navies. *Izmail* would have had ammunition as advanced as any opponent's.

The shells had more than top quality in their favor. In keeping with Russian standards, the 14-inch/52 Pattern 1913 gun fired a hefty shell, 1649 lbs—heavier than any other 14-inch round to see naval service. Mounting twelve guns, *Izmail* thus had a broadside totaling 19,788 lbs. This doesn't simply dwarf *Hindenburg*'s 7152-lb broadside, *it exceeds the broadside of any European battleship ever built*.[51]

The war with Japan had schooled the Russians on the real-world demands of naval combat, including gunnery skills. The sample pool of Russian big-gun marksmanship in World War I, while limited, strongly indicates an excellence in fire control and a consistent performance of the heavy artillery. With all these factors backing her,

---

[51] Other World War I broadsides: *Mackensen* 10,582 lbs; *Bayern* 13,228 lbs; *Queen Elizabeth* 15,360 lbs; *Arizona* and *Fuso* 16,800 lbs. HMS *Nelson* of 1927, the eventual European champ, had 18,432 lbs.

Izmail would likely have delivered a weighty mass of quality ammunition accurately onto her target.

Like all other designs, *Izmail* had shortcomings. Conical barbettes, a dubious arrangement of ammo spaces, a remarkable lack of torpedo protection—and since she never entered service, other bugs may have gone unrevealed.[52] Or maybe the ship would actually have over-achieved. In any case, within the probable range of *Izmail's* performance, there's little doubt that she could have challenged any ship completed for any navy before the Washington Treaty.

Figure 24. The turret arrangement makes *Izmail* look very Russian. (Boris Lemachko Collection)

---

[52] For example, it is only because the 14-inch gun progressed to trials that we know its 2,700 foot/second (f/s) muzzle velocity had to be reduced to 2,400 f/s—in itself, a minor matter. The Russian 12-inch dreadnought gun also had modest muzzle velocity (2,500 f/s). The successful American 16-inch guns of World War II had 2,300-2,500 f/s.

FURTHER READING

Battlecruisers receive lavish exposure in the publishing world, much of it simply retreading the simplistic retrospection of bygone decades. Readers can look forward to strenuous winnowing before finding the wheat, but the following overview may help.

In the 1970s, Siegfried Breyer published his encyclopedic volume on dreadnoughts. With its drawings and technical data and a lengthy overview of the development of armored ships, the book had enough success to earn an English translation (*Battleships and Battle cruisers 1905-1970*)—a treasure trove at that time, yet it can no longer stand as a premier reference amid more recent, more reliable research.

Conway's All the World's Fighting Ships, also getting long in the tooth, still suffices as a starting point, with the first three volumes (covering 1860-1905, 1906-1921, and 1922-1946 respectively) being most relevant. *Conway's* prints the usual statistics, adequate as far as they go, along with some explanatory text. The specialized edition, *Conway's Battleships* (vaguely updated from the aging *All the World's Battleships*), has greater focus if not greater overall value.

Over the years, the quarterly *Warship International* has featured a number of excellent articles (for example, the best treatment of Dutch Design 1047); partial indices are available at the publisher's website.[53] Likewise, the *Warship* journal provides treats for every eager reader; the Dreadnought Project has a complete index.[54] A spin-off of the *Warship* series deserves special mention, the slim paperback *Battle Cruisers* by N. J. M. Campbell, still a valuable resource on British and German ships of World War I despite its age (published 1978). Campbell also wrote *Jutland*, which rates as the ultimate tour of the real-world results when large shells hit large ships.

As might be expected, British battlecruisers have enjoyed the broadest coverage in English-language books. The classic *British Battleships* by Oscar Parkes covers both armored cruisers and battlecruisers, and his armor schematics for pre-dreadnought designs are top-notch. Titles more recent than Parkes (and more accurate for *Dreadnought* and her successors) include R. A. Burt's trilogy (*British Battleships 1889-1904, British Battleships of World War One*, and *British Battleships 1919-1939*) and *British Battleships of World War Two* by Alan Raven and John Roberts. The specifics of battlecruiser fire-control engineering appear in fearless, mind-boggling detail in John Brooks's *Dreadnought Gunnery and the Battle of Jutland*. Perhaps the best single volume on British battlecruisers is the plainly titled *Battlecruisers* by John Roberts, which includes armor schematics and other technical details as well as indispensable background narrative.

Unfortunately, and surprisingly, Germany's "large cruisers" have not received the focus in English that they deserve. Erich Gröner's entries have been translated into English for the first volume of *German Warships 1815-1945*, but the most detailed in-

---

[53] http://www.warship.org/wi_index_intro.htm
[54] http://dreadnoughtproject.org/periodicals/warship.

formation remains inextricably German in such sources as *Große Kreuzer der Kaiserlichen Marine 1906-1918* by Axel Grießmer and various titles from Gerhard Koop and Klaus-Peter Schmolke. Ships of the *Kriegsmarine* era have much better coverage, with the top source being M. J. Whitley's *German Capital Ships of World War Two*. Useful options include the Axis volume of William H. Garzke and Robert O. Dulin's *Battleships* set and, again, books from Koop and Schmolke.

Norman Friedman's *U. S. Cruisers* gives the design histories for *Lexington* and *Alaska*. Garzke and Dulin help with *Alaska*, and Trent Hone has a fine *Lexington* article in *Warship 2011*. However, there is no dedicated volume on the technical and doctrinal development of battlecruisers in America.

A similar situation applies for France. *French Battleships 1922-1956* by John Jordan and Robert Dumas covers all the projects within its scope, but no English sources cover the full range of French thought on battlecruisers.

Other navies suffer even greater neglect. Readers interested in Russia must hunt down articles in *Warship International* and *Warship*, especially those from Stephen McLaughlin. (And his book *Russian and Soviet Battleships* has chapters on *Izmail* and *Sovetskii Soyuz*.) Japan, a hearty believer in battlecruisers, is almost entirely ignored by English-language publishers; at least *Japanese Cruisers of the Pacific War* by Eric Lacroix and Linton Wells covers the B-65 design in some detail, and there is a volume on *Kongo* in the old "Warship Profile" paperback series. As usual, the Italian Navy gets no respect. A solitary English-language book goes deep into Italian dreadnought design, *The Littorio Class* by Bagnasco and de Toro, and the Garzke and Dulin Axis volume has some information. For general information, readers have only the aging *Le navi di linea italiane 1861-1969*.

Research continues into these neglected areas and may yet yield useful results.

Figure 25. Most of *Seydlitz* made it home after Jutland.

www.ingramcontent.com/pod-product-compliance
Lightning Source LLC
Chambersburg PA
CBHW041959100426
42813CB00019B/2935